# WILDERNESS HOMESTEAD

*Helga Rostvit*
*2014*

Helga Gilbertson Rostvit
and Ellen Skoglie Gilbertson

Cover design: Alice Anne Ong

First Printing 2012

Copyright ©2012 Janice and Faye Rostvit. All rights reserved. No part of this book may be used in any manner whatsoever without written permission of the publisher, except in the case of brief quotations in articles and reviews.

For information write:
Chambers College Press
1300 Ninth Street, Greeley, CO 80631
Phone 970-346-1133
Email: chamberscollege@msn.com

ISBN: 978-0-9825659-0-2

# TABLE OF CONTENTS

| | | |
|---|---|---|
| About The Authors | | iv |
| Family Name References | | v |
| What's in a Name | | vi |
| Acknowledgments | | viii |
| Preface | | ix |
| Map | | x |
| 1. | Humble Beginnings | 1 |
| 2. | The Atlantic Crossing | 5 |
| 3. | A Time to Build | 10 |
| 4. | First Winters on the Homestead | 18 |
| 5. | Pioneers on a Harsh Frontier | 26 |
| 6. | Taming the Wilderness | 37 |
| 7. | Sanna Marries Again | 50 |
| 8. | Nass Store and Post Office | 57 |
| 9. | The Great War | 69 |
| 10. | Ma and Pa's Helpers | 79 |
| 11. | More Conveniences Yet Busier Lives | 88 |
| 12. | Tin Lizzie Travel | 95 |
| 13. | Our New Home and Store | 99 |
| 14. | Close Calls | 109 |
| 15. | Christmas Time | 119 |
| 16. | The One-Room School | 123 |
| 17. | Bare Necessities | 129 |
| 18. | Childhood in the North Woods | 136 |
| 19. | Entertaining Ourselves | 145 |
| 20. | A New School | 154 |
| 21. | A Change Within | 163 |
| 22. | Preparing to Serve | 171 |
| 23. | Away from the Homestead | 178 |
| 24. | Mission Work Up North | 184 |
| 25. | Triumphs and Tragedy | 194 |
| 26. | Feeding a Harvest Crew | 197 |
| 27. | Newlyweds and a "Covered Wagon" | 201 |
| 28. | Raising a Family in Wartime | 210 |
| 29. | In Sickness and in Health | 224 |
| 30. | End of an Era | 235 |

## ABOUT THE AUTHORS

**Ellen (Skoglie) Gilbertson** was born to Sanna and Hans Skoglie May 27, 1910. They lived in a log cabin on a homestead in northern Minnesota. Hans was from Norway, Sanna from Sweden. Hans died when Ellen was only five months old. Her mother remarried. Ellen helped her mom with the younger children, one being Helga.

As Ellen had a desire to become a missionary, she attended a Bible college in Kansas City, graduating in 1935. She served with Northern Gospel Mission back in northern Minnesota. She was very effective among the immigrants since she could speak Norwegian and Swedish. In 1936 Ellen married Edward Gilbertson, an immigrant from Norway who was a farmer in North Dakota. They had a son and three daughters: Carl, Elaine, Ruth, and Janice.

Ellen wrote and published several articles, short stories and books including *Road to Galilee*, *Peter the Pioneer*, and *The Way it Was*. She also was in demand as a speaker for many functions in area churches.

**Helga (Gilbertson) Rostvit** was born on the homestead March 31, 1917, the sixth of eight children raised by Scandinavian immigrants, Sanna and John Gilbertson. In 1939, she married Edward Rostvit, also of Norwegian background, who himself had grown up on a homestead. They had four daughters: Laura Jean, Sharon, and twins Janice and Faye.

In 1954, the family moved to Colorado Springs, where Edward helped build the Air Force Academy, then became a millwright, doing precision work with machinery. Helga became a Licensed Practical Nurse in 1960 and enjoyed hospital work for several years. The family loved time in the Rocky Mountains. Helga, together with the twins, hiked several 14,000 foot mountains. Even at age 80 she climbed Pikes Peak.

The Rostvit family have all had trips to Norway and Sweden to visit relatives.

Helga authored the book, *Homesteader's Daughter*.

# FAMILY NAME REFERENCES

**Great Grandparents:**
    John and Helga Anderson (John Gilbertson's father's parents)
    John and Inger Simonson (John Gilbertson's mother's parents)

**Grandparents:**
    Gulbrand and Kari Johnson (John Gilbertson's parents)
    Jonas and Kristina Persson "Jonasson" (Sanna's parents)

**Parents:**
    Father: 1st - Hans Skoglie / 2nd - John Gilbertson
    Mother: Sanna Elise (Jonasdatter, Skoglie) Gilbertson

        Uncles and Aunts:
        Johan "Joe" (brother of John Gilbertson)
        Helge "Harry" (brother of John Gilbertson) and wife Berdetta
        Anders "Andrew" (brother of Sanna) and wife Sarah
        Jonas Kristian "Krist" (brother of Sanna)

**Siblings with birth dates:**     **Siblings' Spouses:**

| # | Sibling | Birth Date | Spouse |
|---|---------|------------|--------|
| 1. | Laura | July 24, 1905 | Paul Rostvit |
| 2. | Johnny | Oct. 25, 1907 | Grace Hackey |
| 3. | Ellen | May 27, 1910 | Edward Gilbertson |
| 4. | Karl | August 4, 1913 | Died unmarried |
| 5. | Inger | May 9, 1915 | Clifford Stahl |
| 6. | Helga | March 31, 1917 | Edward Rostvit |
| 7. | Agnes | June 19, 1918 | Wallace Stahl |
| 8. | Ingvald | June 22, 1920 | Alice Boyle |

**Cousins with birth dates: (Andrew and Sarah Perssons' children)**

1. Johan (in Sweden) 1890
2. Christina   Feb. 4, 1893
3. Helmer   May 26, 1896
4. Anna   July 22, 1900
5. Albert   Oct. 9, 1901
6. Arvid   Oct. 8, 1903
7. Sally   Nov. 16, 1905
8. Carl   Jan. 29, 1907
9. Bertha   Jan. 3, 1910
10. Hilding   Aug. 16, 1912
11. Elva   March 9, 1915

# WHAT'S IN A NAME?

In the past, in both Norway and Sweden, one's surname changed every generation. If a boy's father was Peter, the boy's surname became Peterson - thus, the origin of names such as Hanson, Johnson, Olson. To help identify a person, it was common to tack on their farm name which had a meaning, e.g., Skoglie was from "skog" meaning "forest." The name Rostvit (Rostveit - actual Norwegian spelling) meant a "horse vale or clearing."

Generational name changing was common until the mid-1890s when both Sweden and Norway made a ruling that everyone take a solid surname – either the Anderson, Johnson type, or their farm name. It wasn't that every family agreed on what name to take. An individual could make his own choice.

In our family line, there are some discrepancies or puzzles in regard to people's names:

**Gulbrand and Erik Johnson Holte** were brothers from Norway. With the ruling of taking solid surnames, Gulbrand chose "Johnson" while Erik chose the farm name, "Holte." Gulbrand Johnson was Grandma Kari's first husband. After he died, Kari married his brother, Erik Holte.

**John Gulbrandson** – Helga's father Americanized his name to "Gilbertson."

**Sanna Elise** – Her full name was Susanna Elisabet.

**Grandpa Jonas,** born Sept.14,1848, was the real puzzle. He was Jonas Persson (son of Per.) With the ruling to take a solid surname, Jonas remained the same, but his sons Andrew and Krist, both changed from "Jonasson" to "Persson." Ship manifests, naturalization papers, homestead claims, and even tombstones had all three as Perssons. However, for some reason, all of Jonas' grandchildren knew him as Jonas "Jonasson." Why?? It might be that he took "Jonasson" as a farm name for his homestead to distinguish his place from Andrew Persson's. We don't know. We do know that Grandpa Jonas "Jonasson" Persson, loved the Lord, and his name is in the Lamb's Book of Life. God is not confused – He knows who Jonas is.

### Titles for Grandparents:

Compared to English, the Scandinavian languages have more titles for 'Grandparents.'

There are the general terms:
- "Bestaforeldre" (grandparent)
- "Bestafar" (grandfather)
- "Bestamor" (grandmother)

There are also more specific and endearing titles.

For paternal grandparents:
- "Farfar" (father's father)
- "Farmor" (father's mother)

For maternal grandparents:
- "Morfar" (mother's father)
- "Mormor" (mother's mother)

# ACKNOWLEDGMENTS

From the Editors – Janice and Faye Rostvit

Our mother, Helga Gilbertson Rostvit, wrote *Homesteader's Daughter* published in 1987. Her sister Ellen Skoglie Gilbertson wrote a history called *The Way It Was*, which was printed by her family after her death in 1985. At the time of this publishing, our mother, Helga, is still in good health at age 95. With her blessing and with permission from Ellen's children, Carl, Elaine, Ruth, and Janice, we have combined the narrative from both books, plus have added details and photos which have surfaced since the previous printings. This book has more historical facts of our ancestors who homesteaded in the beginning of the 20th Century.

We appreciate the help from various cousins and second cousins who have sent photos, helpful information, or an additional story. We are especially deeply grateful to Cousin Elaine Peterson (Ellen's daughter) for supplying many of the photos which we did not previously have, and for her hours of research to provide more details of ship manifests, naturalizations, census records, and of what all it took to secure the final proof for establishing a homestead.

We wish to thank various friends who have helped to edit portions of the book. We also thank God for all involved with Chambers College Press. Our heartfelt thanks to Pastor Stephen Ong, and his daughter, Alice, for their expertise and many hours of willing, and selfless labor, with cheerful, optimistic encouragement, to prepare and finalize this manuscript for publishing.

Janice and Faye Rostvit, daughters of Helga

# PREFACE

America was settled by courageous pioneers who came from many faraway lands. Our parents and grandparents were among those hardy folks who left Norway and Sweden, their homelands for untold generations, having said their tearful goodbyes to families and friends whom they would never see again. They came with few possessions, and very little money, speaking only the language of their native land, but with faith in God, they dreamed of a brighter future. They had to face many dangers, beginning with crossing the Atlantic, and followed by unknown hardships as they settled in the remote heavily-timbered areas of northern Minnesota. They carved a living out of the rugged wilderness, surviving illness, near starvation, enduring loneliness, and long, severe winters far from any town.

We, their children, are first-generation Americans, having grown up between two cultures, gaining benefits from both Scandinavia and America. Our generation faced many changes in this country of the New World. We've been blessed to live in a time from the horse and buggy days to the Space Age. This narrative, however, covers the early years, relating a lot of everyday experiences we had while growing up on the homestead.

*-Helga Gilbertson Rostvit*

Editors' Note: *Wilderness Homestead* covers a period of approximately fifty years, 1900-1950, starting with the authors' parents immigrating to America. For much of the earlier years on the homesteads, we have combined the narratives, not indicating whether Helga or Ellen wrote the details. At later times, we indicate which one is writing to relive with them their personal experiences. You will note one difference between the two authors: Ellen calls her parents Ma and Pa, while Helga calls them Mom and Dad. We chose not to change that. We are concluding the narrative with the death of their parents - those early settlers.

Where Scriptures are quoted, we have chosen to use the King James Version, as it would have been the only English version available for use in this time period.

*- Janice and Faye Rostvit*

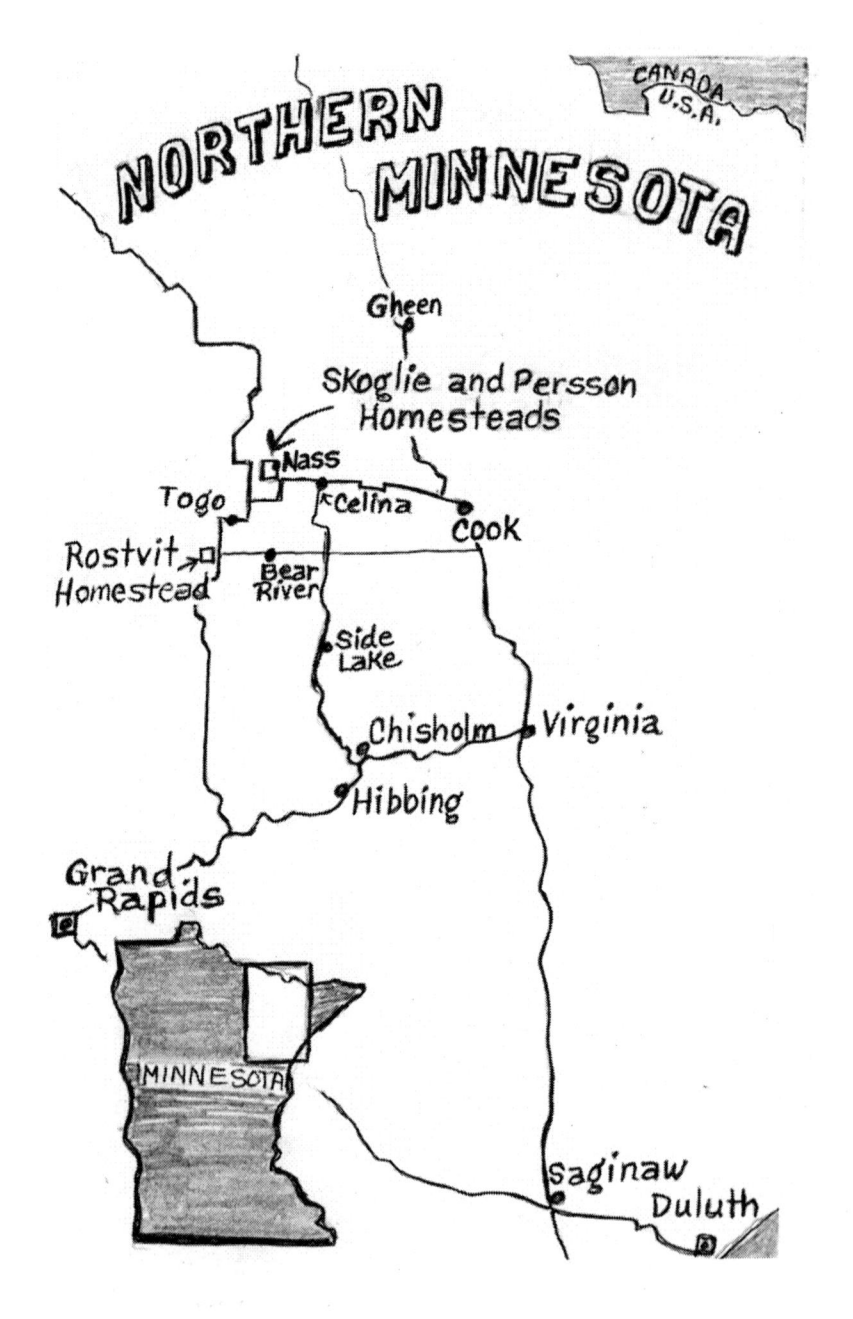

Region of the homestead

## Chapter 1
## HUMBLE BEGINNINGS

The night was cold and the snow lay deep in the wilderness of northern Minnesota. In the pre-dawn darkness of the early morning, March 31, 1917, I had begun to make known that it was time for my entrance into the world.

Sanna turned in bed with a groan and nudged her husband, saying, *"Det er tid! Det er tid!"* (It is time.)

I was to be the sixth child to join the family, so my father didn't question her judgment. He quickly slipped out of bed and lit the kerosene lamp. He dressed and made sure to put some more wood in the stove before waking the children.

There was a hustle and bustle in the log cabin that would soon be my home. My eldest sister, Laura, age 11, hurriedly put on her clothes, then helped to dress Inger who was not quite two. Johnny, age 9, also dressed and went to wake Ellen. When she

PHOTO: March 16, 1913. The log home where we were born. Back: Aunt Sarah and our mother, Sanna. Front: Laura, Ellen, Johnny.

opened her eyes she saw Johnny grinning at her, but she scowled in return. She was puzzled by all the commotion in the cabin. She saw Laura helping Inger. She saw Karl, age three-and-a-half, who was struggling into his union suit - that is, long winter underwear. Then she noticed that her mother wasn't up yet.

With a tone of urgency, Johnny said, "Get up, Ellen! We need to walk to Grandpa's house." He and Laura knew what was happening, but six-year-old Ellen did not.

**Ellen writes her recollections of that day.**

I could not understand why we had to leave when Mama could stay there so comfortable in her nice warm bed! I wanted to protest, but thought better of it. Pa continued to rush about with no explanation. *"Skynd deg nå,"* (Hurry up now!) he said, as he helped the smaller ones put on their coats, mittens and hats. He lit a lantern and stepped out into the bitter cold to bring a sled close to the door. Shortly he came back in.

He dashed to Ma's bedside and whispered something. [He reassured Sanna he would return as soon as possible.] Then he turned toward us children and lifted the two youngest, Karl and Inger, into his arms, *"Nå skal vi gå. Johnny, åpne døran, vær så snil."* (Now let's go. Johnny, open the door, please.)

We all slipped outside as Johnny held the door, and made sure to close it behind us. I gasped as I breathed in the snappy cold air. Pa situated both Karl and Inger in the box of the sled, tucking a blanket around them. Now he could pull them and still carry the lantern.

We headed out, going southwest, Pa leading the way. The packed snow near the cabin crunched beneath our feet in the sub-zero temperatures. I still pondered why we needed to trudge half a mile through the deep snow to our grandparents' home while it was still dark. I whined, *"Men, vi har ikke hadde mat ennå,"* (But, we haven't eaten yet.)

Laura explained, *"Vi skal har mat med Bestamor."* (We'll eat with Grandma). That silenced me for a while as I envisioned Swedish pancakes floating in blueberries and cream.

When we got into the deeper snow which covered the field, the going was tougher. Laura, Johnny and I struggled along behind the sled. We kept sinking into snowdrifts. Laura and Johnny were managing to keep up with the sled, but I could not. I envied Karl and Inger who were riding, all wrapped up like mummies. As the lantern swayed with Pa's determined steps, it cast eerie shadows. I tried to hurry, but repeatedly sank into the snow. Since my legs were shorter than the others, it was difficult to pull myself out. Finally I was completely stuck. I panicked as I tried to get up, but only sank deeper, plus got snow in my woolen mittens. Realizing I was being left behind in the darkness, I screamed out in terror. I thought I saw a wolf behind every tree in the gloom of early dawn. [Ellen's fears were not as far-fetched as it might seem, for there were numerous wolves in that wilderness. Their father was a bit impatient with the children for he was worrying about his wife being left alone. He was eager to leave the children with their grandparents.]

Pa did stop and came back to lift me out of the snowdrift. He brushed the snow off of me, shook the snow out of my mittens, and pulled the woolen scarf back up over my nose and mouth. Then he urged Laura and Johnny to walk behind me so they could help me if I got stuck again. I did get stuck a couple more times, and I thought they would pull my arms out of their sockets to free me.

Finally we neared the cabin. Lights from the window reflected on the snow. Grandpa Jonas and Grandma Kristina were always up early. He already had put wood in the stoves, and Grandma had the coffee pot on the range. When she heard us coming, she opened the door to welcome us.

Pa carried Karl and Inger in, as *Mormor* (literally "mother's mother") helped us to shed our coats and mittens. Pa then turned to leave, saying to Grandma, "I'll be going by Andrew's place to get Sarah. She promised she would help when the time came."

Mormor nodded understandingly.

It puzzled me a great deal that Pa didn't even have time to stay for a cup of coffee and some of Grandma's good sour-cream cookies. *Why was he in such a hurry? Why stop at Uncle Andrew's place? That's way out of the way.* Everyone seemed to know what it was all about except me – and of course the two younger ones, but they weren't puzzling over it like I was.

I enjoyed the good meals, and the coffee and cookies between meals, but the day was dreadfully long. After sitting and paging through the Sears Roebuck, Montgomery Ward, and M.W. Savage catalogs, there wasn't much to do except stare through the east window and wait for Pa to come and take us home.

Laura was rocking Inger to sleep in the big homemade rocker, and Grandma was chatting with a neighbor who had dropped in for coffee. I do not recall that *"Bestafar"* (Grandfather) was around much that day except at mealtime. Probably he was out feeding the cattle and cutting wood. My big brother seemed to know the reason for our early evacuation from home. He had that smug grin on his freckled face.

Late in the afternoon, Pa finally returned and brought us home. I was totally surprised when I saw Helga Margareta for the first time. *"Å! Har vi en ny søster!"* (Oh! We have a new sister!)

Johnny's grin spread from ear to ear as he said, "You should have known there would be a new baby in the house, Ellen. Didn't you remember when Inger was born and we were sent outside and weren't permitted to go in for dinner at noon?" I did remember that day nearly two years earlier. At the time, when Laura brought sandwiches and milk out to us for dinner, I had thought they were cleaning house. She often shooed us out of the house when she helped Ma with the cleaning.

\* \* \* \*

By the time of Helga's birth, Sanna had been in America thirteen years. She loved her family. As she cradled an infant, marveling at new life, it was as it were, a fulfillment of the hope she had clung to when leaving Sweden - a dream of new beginnings. Life was not easy, yet she faced it with courage and resilience because of her faith in God.

PHOTO: Three-month-old Helga with sister Inger, age 2.

## Chapter 2
## THE ATLANTIC CROSSING

Our parents emigrated from the Scandinavian countries. America was advertising its need for immigrants to come and settle the vast wilderness areas of the north. Free land was given to immigrants, who otherwise received no government assistance. They had to file for their 160 acre homestead and endure the hardships and dangers of developing the land. After proving the land for five years, and finalizing paperwork, it was legally theirs.

Our mother, Sanna Elise Jonasdatter (Jonas' daughter) was born July 24, 1883. [She was named Susanna Elisabet, but later she preferred to be called Sanna or Elise.] She grew up near the town of Gäddede, in Jamtland, a region in northern Sweden. This inland, hilly area was heavily forested and had many lakes. The harsh winter climate was much like that of northern Minnesota. For many centuries Jamtland had been a part of Norway. When Sweden seized it, around the close of the 17th century, they treated the people cruelly, for some time not even giving them privileges as normal citizens. Therefore, much of the populace still considered themselves as Norwegians, or at least were proud of their Norwegian heritage. It is interesting that in the ship manifest of our maternal ancestors, they claimed themselves to be from the nation of Sweden, but their ethnicity "Norwegians."

The family lived by a lake on a tree-covered peninsula. They didn't own any property, but worked for other landowners. The peninsula was near the town of Gäddede, which is situated

PHOTO: Peninsula in Sweden where my mother's family lived.

very close to Norway's eastern border. In September of 1903 the family was making plans to move to America. Sanna's parents, Jonas, age 54, and Kristina, 56, together with their youngest son, Jonas Kristian, (called "Krist,") would be leaving first. Later they would help sponsor their other two children, married son Andrew and twenty-year-old Sanna to emigrate.

PHOTO - 1903: The family leaves their home on the peninsula, as three of them prepare to leave Sweden. Seated in the wagon are Sanna and her mother, Kristina. The men standing are Sanna's brothers Andrew, and Krist, and Sanna's father, Jonas Persson.

The whole family helped pack up their belongings for leaving their home on the peninsula. They first went to Gäddede where Sanna was left with Andrew's wife and children.

Andrew then led the horse as he and those emigrating headed westward toward Norway's border. Sanna waved as the wagon slowly rolled out of sight. It was heart-wrenching to watch them leave, but she clung to the hope that eventually she, too, would be with them in America.

For those with the wagon, it was a long, slow 200 mile journey. On September 14, while en route, Jonas had his 55th birthday. Upon reaching the docks at Norway's coastal town of Trondheim, Andrew helped his parents and brother to get their trunks and belongings on board the ship. After bidding them farewell, he drove the wagon back to Gäddede to join his family.

Meanwhile, Jonas, Kristina and son, Krist, sailed south to Liverpool, England, where they boarded the ship Ivernia. Their ship docked in Boston on September 30, and the threesome went by train to northern Minnesota.

In Sweden, Sanna secured a job with a family who needed a house servant. She received such small wages, that she could save very little. The work was hard. There was the usual cooking, washing dishes, and house cleaning. She would have preferred her work of past summers when she was a shepherdess in peaceful high pastures.

One day she was sharply ordered to wash clothes. They took Sanna to the attic. There was a mountain of dirty bed linens and woolen socks. This was the previous winter's laundry! It was customary to pile up the dirty clothes in winter, and wash them in the springtime, but this was now September! Why hadn't they done that laundry in the spring? To add to her difficulty, Sanna was treated harshly. Yet she endured, keeping in mind an exhortation from Scripture, *"Servants, be subject to your masters with all fear; not only to the good and gentle, but also to the froward[obstinate]. For this is thankworthy, if a man for conscience toward God endure grief, suffering wrongfully.... if, when ye do well, and suffer for it, ye take it patiently, this is acceptable with God."* (I Pet. 2:18-20b).

PHOTO: Gäddede, in Jamtland, Sweden

Whenever Sanna felt lonely, she kept in mind the promise her father and brother had made - that they would work hard and not only make a living, but would save money for her passage. She dreamed of joining them in the New World.

It was the following spring of 1904, when Sanna received the letter with her passage money. She was elated, not having anticipated it coming so soon. Her father and Krist had worked on the construction of the Great Northern Railroad for the unheard of wages of a dollar-a-day each. In the letter, her father stated that together with her mother, they would be waiting for her to arrive at the train station in Duluth, Minnesota.

Sanna was eager to start on her journey. It had been a long winter for her and she had missed her family very much. The thought of being with them again, filled her heart with joy! It was early April when Andrew took his sister to the docks at Trondheim. At that time, however, there were so many people emigrating that there were not enough ships to take them to America. When Sanna was informed that it might be a long time before there would be a berth available on a passenger ship, she, together with some others, opted not to wait. Instead, they booked passage on an old, refurbished cattle boat. They had stops in Glasgow, Scotland, and Liverpool, England, before heading across the Atlantic in their ship called the Pomeranian.

Sanna was enjoying the voyage, together with many other young folks. There was camaraderie – all had embarked on a wonderful adventure. What fun they were having! Then came a storm on the ocean, and there was no more joking or laughter. With the rough seas, the ship was lifted to the crest of the huge waves. Then as the billows rolled from beneath the hull, the craft would crash down to the bottom of the next swell. Over and over again the old ship was carried up and down, up and down, and was mercilessly battered by the mountainous waves. The passengers grew sick - so sick that some thought they were going to die. Every heart was gripped by fear when the old vessel creaked and groaned, threatening to fall apart. Water sloshed in through the open portholes and through the gutters behind the former cow stalls. As the ship listed, water ran out again, carrying with it boots, shoes, socks, hats, small suitcases and other articles that fell to the floor during the storm. At last the skies brightened, the storm subsided, and the seas calmed. Some folks who had been deathly ill steadily improved, but many remained weak and emotionally shaken from their ordeal.

On April 22, 1904, the ship docked in Boston, then went on to Halifax, Nova Scotia, where Sanna disembarked. There, she boarded a train with Canadian Pacific Railroad and headed westward. She entered the United States at Sault Ste. Marie in Upper Michigan, then passed through Wisconsin to Duluth, Minnesota. Her parents and brother, Krist, were there to meet her and to take her to Saginaw, which was about 20 miles to the west. What a joyous reunion they had that day! They talked far into the night about all that had happened to them since they were last together.

The day after she arrived, Sanna was surprised to see an old acquaintance. It was Hans Martin Skoglie, a tall 30-year-old man from Nordlie, Norway, just across the border from Gäddede. At one time he had dated Sanna's older sister, Brita, but then she died of TB while in her teens. Hans had actually crossed the Atlantic on the same ship as Sanna's parents and brother. The family readily accepted him as a friend from the "old country." For the past months Hans had been working on the same railroad crew as Jonas and Krist. He was a hard worker, yet in nature, there was a shy, soft-spoken way about him. A friendship began to develop with Sanna.

## Chapter 3
## A TIME TO BUILD

Hans and Jonas made two trips into Duluth. The first was to the District Court to fill out papers which showed their intention to become citizens of the United States. A copy of that legal paper was needed when, two days later, August 15, 1904, they went to the Land Office of the Department of the Interior. With eager anticipation, this was the day they were applying for homesteads. In Hans' paperwork, he declared, "I am a single man above the age of 21 years and have declared my intention to become a citizen of the United States. My application is honestly and in good faith made for purposes of actual settlement and cultivation."

Although the land would be free, there was a $14 charge for the paperwork for each of them - two week's wages. Without having seen the land, Jonas and Hans came away with the legal right to homestead two quarters of a mile section in the northeastern area of Itasca County. Returning to Saginaw, the men eagerly shared the good news with Kristina and Sanna.

It had not taken a long courtship for Sanna and Hans to know that they were meant for each other. In October of 1904, the 21-year-old girl from Jamtland, and the man who had grown up just across the border in Norway were married. Their hearts were filled with rosy dreams for the future as they began their young lives together in a little tarpaper shack at the railroad camp at Saginaw. They never imagined what hardships they would endure as pioneers in the wilderness.

Later that month, they all moved to Hibbing so the men could find work in the open pit iron ore mine during the coldest part of the winter. Before securing jobs, however, the three men, Jonas, Hans and Krist, eager to check out their homesteads, walked forty miles north. They trekked for many hours. At dusk, when they were nearing their allotted acreage, they came upon an abandoned log cabin. The cabin had no floor, and its walls had cracks between the logs, but the roof was good and there were two rusty, but usable stoves. They spent the night there and were delighted over this good fortune. This would be a shelter to which they could come the following spring when they would arrive to settle their claims. It could be their temporary dwelling while building their own cabins.

The next day, the men located their section. They walked to and fro across their 160 acre claims, marveling that they could own such property. That is, they would own it after five years if they remained and proved up the site. They had been poor peasants in the "old country" laboring for those who were land owners, but now they felt as rich as kings. Jonas' claim bordered the south side of what would become his son, Andrew's homestead. The Skoglies' property would be to the east of Andrew's. On the border between the Skoglies' land and Andrew Persson's was a lovely birch and pine-studded graduation of rocky hills. They called it the *"fjelle"* (mountain). It would become a popular picnic area for the clan. The men studied the layout of the land, contemplating where they might build their homes. As it was getting dark, the men returned to the abandoned cabin. They spent the night there again before making the long hike back to Hibbing.

PHOTO: A later photo (1913) looking south from the top of the *"fjelle."* Hans Skoglie's homestead to the left, and Andrew Persson's homestead seen through the trees in the snowy clearing to the right (west.)

During the winter months, while the men worked in the mine, their thoughts were continually on all they would need to buy before they would make the actual move to their homesteads. They could not yet afford to buy horses and wagons of their own, but there were men in Hibbing who, for a fee, would transport immigrants to their homesteads.

Early in March of 1905, the Perssons and Skoglies packed their belongings for the trip northward: clothing and personal items, bedding, cooking supplies, dishes, food, lanterns and kerosene, a wash board, a spinning wheel, seeds for planting, plus all the tools the men would need for building cabins. In Hibbing they purchased one wood-burning cook stove, a pot-bellied heating stove, stove pipes, windows, and hardware.

It was good to make the trip near the end of winter. There would still be snow in the woods, but the ground was still frozen, so the rough wagon roads were solid enough for transporting heavy loads, and would not be all mud. There was no room for passengers, unless one was allowed to ride beside the teamster. The rest walked. They traveled between fifteen and twenty miles that first day to a place called Side Lake. Other newcomers who were settled there invited them to stay over night, and they gratefully accepted the hospitality. The next day, March 9th, they continued their journey and reached the deserted cabin at dusk.

The men cut and carried wood into the cabin so they could start fires in both of the stoves. Although the days were gradually getting milder, it was still winter. Sanna and her mother busied themselves stuffing twisted hay into the cracks between the logs to keep out the cold. The hay had been carried in from a little log barn that was close to the abandoned cabin. While the women weather-proofed the cabin, the men were cutting and dragging in spruce boughs and arranging them in the corners to cover the dirt floor where they would bed down. They then put hay on the spruce boughs so there would be padding under their blankets for sleeping. All this was done while the fires in the stoves were crackling cheerily. When the stoves were hot enough, Kristina and her daughter set to work preparing their late supper.

The trip had taken two long, tiring days over rough terrain, including rocks and tree stumps. Sanna in particular was more exhausted than she had ever been before, for she was "in the family way," as it was modestly expressed in those days. After supper, the family happily retired to their spruce-bough beds.

Although they all were weary, they anticipated with excitement the days and weeks ahead, of their pioneer lives now begun in America's untamed wilderness.

The following morning after breakfast, Jonas, his teenage son Krist, and his son-in-law Hans, set out for their claims, carrying their tools. Axes, saws, hammers, picks, shovels, and other small tools were the only building equipment they needed. The raw material was growing on their own homesteads.

There was a natural meadow on the Skoglie homestead and a small stream meandered its way through it. They assumed the meadow may have been formed by a forest fire. The fact that most of the trees on that part of the land were young growths seemed to verify their theory that a fire had burned the trees not too many years earlier. Since poplars grow fast, there was an abundance of them. Some were tall, straight and large enough for building cabins. The birch were young and slender. The spruce and balsam were small, but several tall jack pines grew on the eastern edge of the claim. There were also two tall Norway pines that lifted their heads high above the scrubby growth that surrounded them.

The three men set to work, cutting logs for a cabin. They agreed to build Jonas and Kristina's cabin first. They wanted it large enough to house all of them comfortably while they would build the Skoglie cabin. It would be 16' x 18' plus would have a 7' x 14' kitchen. The work was hard – felling the timber, peeling the bark off the logs, then measuring and cutting deep notches near the ends to fit snugly for the corners. They also cut down some cedar trees from which they would split some long shakes – thin at one end and thick at the other for roof shingles. Sawing some planks for flooring would be the last challenge. They rigged up a platform or scaffolding so one man could stand on top and another below to cut the planks with a two-man saw. They needed boards not only for the floor but also for making a door, and window frames.

After a few weeks with daily encouraging progress, the cabin appeared to be nearing completion. Its walls were up. Its roof was on. Its door was hung. Its three, small two-paned windows were set in. They also planned to put in a steep, narrow staircase to an attic-type loft where they could sleep. They had a hand planer, but the work to make the boards smooth was discouragingly tedious. Finally they determined to leave the floor planks in a rough state. They could take more time to make smooth boards when building their cupboards, shelves, tables, and beds. The men worked steadily to finish enough of the floor boards for getting the cook stove set into place. After that, whatever flooring they would get finished would be for storing some of their boxes and trunks.

One day, the owner of their temporary dwelling returned. The man did not react angrily, but rather was pleased to find them there, and to learn that they would be his close neighbors. He was an immigrant from Germany, but had been in this country long enough to speak the language quite fluently. Hans had picked up a workable knowledge of English while working on the railroad and in the mines, so they managed to communicate.

PHOTO: Jonas and Kristina Persson by their homestead cabin built in 1905

Jonas and his family felt awkward about staying any longer in the man's cabin now that he had returned. Even though the man urged them to stay, the family immediately moved to their own cabin. Although it still lacked much of its flooring planks, it was far more livable than their borrowed temporary home.

Outdoor work was impeded by constant rains that persisted into early summer. If it was raining, they worked indoors laying more of the floor boards. When the showers would let up, the men felled timber for building a second cabin, a 15' x 20' one for the Skoglies. It had one door, and two windows. Finally Hans and Sanna moved into their floorless cabin while the rains were still coming in sudden showers day and night. They were very happy to have their own home on their own land. Whenever it rained, a little stream would creep in under one corner of the logs and angle its way to the far corner, making a regular creek bed across the earthen floor. To avoid the mud, Sanna would then climb up on the wood-framed bunk. One can safely assume that there wasn't much housework for her to have to do.

At first she had no stove for cooking. If she wanted to bake bread, she would walk the half mile through the woods to her parent's home to use her mother's oven. Many days the two of them would eat their main meal at her folks' home. Otherwise, Sanna would build a fire in a hollow stump outside. Sometimes a sudden shower would extinguish her fire before the coffee in the blackened gallon pail had come to a boil. Yet when she talked about it, she always laughed, never thinking of it as a hardship, but rather as the greatest time of her life.

That first summer on the homestead was a very busy one. Besides the cabin building, there were wells to dig, a garden patch to spade up and plant. Then the men would need to make a root cellar – a "root house" as they called it - for each place, so that in the fall their garden produce could be safely stored away and accessible during the long winter months. They also planned to put up some of the coarse wild hay from the meadow as they had dreams of acquiring at least one cow for the two households. Of course, cutting and stacking enough wood for winter fuel was another essential! Sanna had not been idle while the men labored at their tasks. She enjoyed working outside. In the late spring, even though she was with child, she helped to clear brush and to prepare a plot of ground for a garden.

During rain showers when they were forced indoors, Hans set to work putting a floor in their cabin. Sanna sat on the bunk sewing or knitting baby clothes and counting the days until their blessed event. The time came in the middle of that busy summer of 1905. It was right on Sanna's 22nd birthday, July 24th, that she gave birth to their first child, Laura Christina. After the birth, Sanna took a few days off from raking hay, stacking wood, or working in the garden.

Later that summer the men walked to Hibbing to welcome Andrew Persson and his family who were arriving from Sweden. While in town, they purchased a cook stove for the Skoglies, plus supplies needed for building Andrew's cabin. Then they returned by hiring some wagons. There was great rejoicing when they arrived back at the homesteads. Their joy was tinged with sadness, however, as only five of the Perssons' six children were with them. Their eldest son, Johan, had remained in Sweden.

Andrew explained the situation why the 14-year-old had been left behind. It seems the Swedish government was concerned that so many young men were leaving the country to move to America. Sweden was industrializing at the time and needed more young men to work in their factories, and also to serve in the military. Therefore, local officials in all communities were commissioned to put pressure on young men to stay in Sweden. In Gäddede, the Lutheran priest was the man to serve as the government's agent. He was the one who kept all birth, marriage and death records, plus land transactions or disputes. Now government officials had pressured him to turn in names of ones whom he would dissuade from leaving the country.

As Andrew and his family were making their final preparations to emigrate, the priest had come to them and said, "You must leave Johan here. He hasn't been confirmed yet. You wouldn't want to put him in jeopardy, would you? If your ship were to sink, Johan wouldn't go to heaven." With that guilt trip being put on them, Andrew and Sarah felt forced to comply. They left Johan with relatives, but assured him they would send money for his passage after he had been confirmed. As Andrew related the story, his parents were much relieved that Johan would be immigrating later. Little did they know, he never would be coming.

*[Decades later, through relatives in Sweden, we learned the reason why.]*

In 1907, two years after his parents and siblings had left the country, Johan received the money sent him for his ship's passage. He was sixteen years old and was eager to travel to America. Having neither a horse nor wagon, Johan faced a dilemma. How would he get to the coast? Finally he determined to walk the more than 200 miles over the ranges and through the valleys to Trondheim. By the time he arrived, he was weak, tired, and hungry. He fainted as he boarded the ship. The ship's doctor, having concluded that the youth was unfit to travel, then refused him passage.

Greatly disheartened, Johan walked back to Sweden. He still wanted to join his family in America, so he got jobs, mostly timber work, to save more money. Then he met a young lady with whom he fell in love. In 1915 when Johan was 24, they married. By that time his parents had been gone for ten years and had a total of eleven children, five of whom Johan had never met. Still desiring to immigrate to America, Johan assumed that he and his bride could make the trip. He talked of his dream to his wife. As she listened, however, mental images created by the reports of the 1912 ill-fated maiden voyage of the Titanic terrified her. Even more recently than that, another ship of immigrants had sunk. Although all of its passengers were rescued, the news of those two tragedies were too fresh in her mind. Her reaction was final, "I will never set foot on a ship!!" So, we finally learned why Johan stayed in Sweden.

## Chapter 4
## FIRST WINTERS ON THE HOMESTEAD

Andrew's family moved in with his parents. On November 16, 1905, his wife Sarah gave birth to their seventh child, Sally. The cabin was nearly bursting at the seams with five adults and six children. Shortly after Sally was born, the three men, Jonas, Hans, and Andrew, walked the forty miles to Hibbing to spend the remainder of the fall and all of the winter months working in the mines. They hated to leave their families, but they needed to earn money for supplies, especially staples like flour, sugar, oatmeal, coffee, salt, and rice.

Krist, now age 20, was left at the homesteads so he could help the women at both households while the rest of the men were gone. He would do the men's chores of splitting wood to keep enough kindling ready for the stoves – keeping the home fires burning - while the women kept the spinning wheels humming and the knitting needles clicking.

Her parents' home was much roomier than Sanna's, yet it still seemed crowded at times to the two women who kept house. Christina, age 12, the eldest of Sarah's six children in the house, brought the younger ones downstairs in the morning. It was she who made their breakfast and tried to keep them from being rowdy or upsetting their grandmother.

Sanna was lonely while Hans was away, but she had many things to do, so time passed quickly. Laura was a happy, healthy baby and it took a lot of time just to feed, bathe, and change her, but it was a delight to watch her grow. She gurgled and cooed most of the time. With Hans gone, Sanna needed someone to help. It was decided that Helmer, who was age nine, would spend the winter at the Skoglie home. Not only would he learn responsibilities, but also it made his grandparents' cabin a little less crowded. Sanna enjoyed his company and his help.

Helmer must have been rather a precocious child because he could read so well that he devoured anything and everything. He had probably only had two years of schooling before they left Sweden because children were not accepted in public schools there until age seven. Their family only had a few books with them, so he read the same material several times. He was thrilled to see that Sanna had a Swedish magazine, *"Kvinnan och Hjemmet"* (Women and the Home). She gave him permission to read it, and he eagerly read every story and article.

Helmer was good with the baby. When Sanna had work to do outside, she didn't have to worry about leaving the baby alone since he was there. She was very grateful for his help, and she loved to get out of the cabin for fresh air. Many hours per week were spent chopping wood, even though the small log woodshed was stacked to the eaves from their summer work. Then, too, Sanna had a snare line to check each morning, after which she would skin and clean her catch and prepare the meals. There was an abundance of snowshoe rabbits. They left clear trails as they hopped through the woods and across the snowy meadows. The pioneers enjoyed the fresh meat with which they made delicious stews, meatballs, and soups.

Christmas was a lonely time for everyone without the men. Since the miners were given only one day off for the holiday, they couldn't get home. The families could not afford the traditional lutefisk - a specially prepared codfish that all Scandinavians enjoy for Christmas dinner. They looked forward to another year for that special treat when the men could be at home also. For this first Christmas on their claims, rabbit stew would have to suffice, yet they did not complain. They were thankful that they did have enough to eat. Their root cellar had been filled that fall with many bushels of potatoes, rutabagas, turnips and carrots, yet with so many mouths to feed, the supplies diminished continually. Potatoes could be used in many ways. The flour supply was used sparingly. The women had loaf sugar for their coffee, and the children were permitted a light sprinkling of sugar on their oatmeal, but when Christmas came, they splurged by baking cookies, making flat bread and lefse, and even using a few raisins in the Christmas Eve rice porridge. [Lefse, made from a dough of potatoes, flour, milk and butter, was rolled very thin and lightly browned using the surface of the wood range.]

A small spruce tree was brought in and the children had fun stringing cranberry garlands, or making some paper chains to decorate the tree. The Swedish Bible was opened to read the story of Jesus' birth. Grandpa Jonas was the one who usually read Scripture when they had Sunday School lessons in the home. Now they missed his authoritative, yet loving voice. Uncle Krist assumed the role, and did it well. Everyone joined in to sing Christmas carols. The favorite was *"Gledelig Jul, Helige Jul"* (Glad Christmas, Holy Christmas or "Silent Night.") Gifts for the children were hand-knitted scarves and mittens. Each of the women kept a brave face, but inwardly their thoughts were on their husbands. What a lonely Christmas Eve and Christmas Day they must be having in that far-off mining town! Surely they were yearning for their families. They were consoled with thoughts of Jesus' birth. What of Mary's parents back in far-off Nazareth. They must have felt the same yearnings of separation when their loved ones, including a grandchild, Jesus, were in Bethlehem. Yet, God was with them and yes, truly He was with Mary and Joseph. *"Behold, a virgin shall conceive, and bear a son, and shall call his name Immanuel, 'God with us.'"* (Isaiah 7:14) *"And the Word was made flesh, and dwelt among us, (and we beheld his glory the glory as of the only begotten of the Father,) full of grace and truth."* (John 1:14)

Kristina, Sarah, and Sanna also knew that their husbands were godly men. They would be praying for their families. They all took time during their Christmas celebrations to pray for the menfolk. They could survive this temporary separation, knowing God was in control.

Christmas passed and as 1906 was ushered in with more winter storms, the snow continued to pile higher in the swamps and across the little meadows and clearings. The wolves howled closer and closer to the cabins.

One morning, Sanna went out as usual to check her snare line. As she came to the edge of a clearing, she heard snuffling, and snarling sounds in the heavily wooded and brushy areas near her. "Lord, help me," she whispered, as she quickly retreated into the open space, yet the threatening sounds seemed even closer. She dared not turn her back on them but walked backward, being careful not to lose her balance in the snow. Her eyes darted back and forth, scanning the edge of the forest as she moved steadily back. Shadowy forms flitted among the trees, but they did not come out into the open. Sanna breathed a sigh of relief when at last she reached the cabin. After that she was quite content to confine her activities closer to the security of her home.

The wood supply dwindled down, but there was enough to last until spring. The frozen rabbit meat that she kept in a large crock in the woodshed, however, soon diminished to a few soup bones. She hoped there would be a mild spell in late February or early March. Then another cold spell would freeze a hard crust on the surface and the wolves could *"spring på skara"* (run on the hard crust) to go after larger game rather than going after rabbits. Sanna would then be free to set her snares again.

Springtime came with some heavy rainstorms. The snows of winter were giving way to water, and mud. One evening, before the men had returned from Hibbing, three strangers appeared at the door of Sanna's cabin. Rain was pouring down steadily. The men were soaked. Sanna immediately invited them in, understanding that they were hungry and weary. They spoke very few words of the American language and she herself could speak very little, but young Helmer caught some of the meaning in their faltering words and gestures. They had claims five miles west of the Skoglie homestead. They wanted a place to stay for the night and would go on to their claims in the morning. Sanna made supper for them of potatoes and vegetables and gave them the few slices of bread she had. They enjoyed eating their supper and standing by the stove to dry off before curling up on the floor to sleep. The men were immigrants from Russia who no doubt had been working in the mines. That same summer they settled on their claims. At least two of them became the most prosperous farmers in the area.

Finally, Jonas, Hans, and Andrew returned home. That

summer the men busied themselves putting up a good-sized two-room cabin for Andrew and Sarah's family. They also erected a small barn, a woodshed, and a "root house." Somehow that summer they got some chickens and three cows – one for each homestead. Sanna was happy to have her brother Andrew nearby. He was a kind, gentle, quiet man, and was always there if someone needed him. Sanna also considered Sarah to be her best friend. The world was so much brighter when they could discuss their problems or joys over a cup of good strong coffee!

PHOTO: Andrew and Sarah Persson by their cabin built in 1906

That fall of '06, the men walked to Hibbing for their second winter of working in the mines. They worked for a few weeks, but there was much violence in the mining towns. Labor organizing factions were trying to force miners to form a union. When the three men realized there was little hope of any more work for some time, they decided to go home. December 21 they filled their packs with what staple foods they could afford, plus a few gifts for Christmas, then hiked back to the peaceful quiet of their homesteads. Being midwinter, it was a tiring trek. Their families were happy to have their menfolk back for the winter, but especially overjoyed that they arrived home in time for Christmas.

Since the three families were left without the income that the men previously earned in the mines, they had a smaller supply of flour. The following summer, 1907, they tried raising small fields of wheat and rye so they could make their own flour. They did get a harvest. The only drawback was that their hand-cranked gristmills made very coarse flour. Nevertheless, it made an excellent porridge for breakfast or supper. [In fact, years later, they were still making their own cracked wheat cereal. One time two roving reporters from the cities were in the area. Sanna told them that she had just prepared a kettleful of home-ground wheat porridge. They were so hungry that they ate and raved about the good taste. Of course, no doubt, there was rich milk or cream to pour on it. The reporters stayed the night and also were served breakfast before they left. Later they wrote an article about their sojourn in pioneer country and the nourishing and tasty supper and breakfast they had enjoyed.]

Their summer was busy, as all summers would be, with so many tasks that had to be done before facing another winter. After the work of planting the potatoes, other vegetables, and the wheat and rye, came the hoeing, or pulling weeds. Besides gardening, there was haying, feeding animals, milking cows, or cutting brush and trees to clear more land. The trees were cut into stove lengths with bucksaws and piled to dry for winter fuel. Andrew made some trips to Duluth to sign up for his homestead. Sanna, who turned twenty-six in July, was "in the family way" again, yet she carried on helping with the work along with everyone else. She was happy that Sarah was close at hand when her time would come.

Although many hopeful, enthusiastic pioneers came to settle their claims, many returned to the state or town from which they had come, long before they had fulfilled the five-year live-on period that gave them the title right to ownership of their 160 acres. The German man in whose unfinished cabin the five of Jonas and Kristina's family had stayed when they came to the area, remained there only for the summer. Sanna did not see him again until a few years later when he suddenly appeared as a kind of census taker. He walked from homestead to homestead to record the names of the children of whom there was no birth record. Even at only a few cents a head he made a living that summer. He disappeared again. No one knew where he lived.

One young couple, planning to establish a store in the region, built a long log building beside their cabin. They brought merchandise in on a temporary railroad which was constructed for some logging in the area. Soon there would be the unbelievable convenience of a grocery and general supply store only ten miles south of the pioneering Perssons' clan.

On October 15, only Jonas and Andrew walked to Hibbing to find employment again in the iron ore mine. They noted that the new store they had heard about was ready for business. Having trusted it would be ready, they had left some cash with Krist so that later in winter, he and Helmer could take a sled to the new store to buy some needed staples.

In the meantime, Hans waited for the important event of their second child's birth. He was overjoyed when on October 25, John Martin was born. He had a son! Only a few days after the birth, he left to join the other men. Sanna's heart was heavy to see him go. It would be another long winter, and she thought of how much she and little Laura would miss him. She also wished Hans could watch the growth of his infant son.

Before the first good sledding snows had settled down enough to be able to pull a heavily-loaded sled easily, the supplies of sugar, rice, flour, and coffee already were running low. Even though the going would be tough, Uncle Krist, age 22, and Helmer, 13, headed out. They trudged through the snow, pulling their sled. The ten miles seemed a long way, but they looked forward to having a little rest at the store before returning home with their load. When at last they reached the clearing where the store should have been, they stopped and stared open-mouthed. They only saw a snow-covered, twisted heap of burned rubble. As they drew near, they kicked at the charred logs that protruded from the snow. Then they sat and rested on their sled awhile before making the long walk back without the sugar, rice, flour and coffee – and the candy they hoped would have been included free.

In the meantime, the men working in Hibbing, had learned about that store burning down. The owner and his wife had moved back to Hibbing where he found work in the mines. The three men were concerned for their families, but not unduly worried. They knew that the women were capable of managing with what they had on hand. They prayed that God would console their wives and watch over them.

The pioneer women did have a tough time to stretch out their scant supplies, but as the men had assumed, they did manage. They learned to live without their morning and afternoon coffee. There wasn't even enough for breakfast. They decided to save what was left for Christmas. They had some oatmeal that helped to extend what flour remained, but mostly they used potatoes, making potato starch. Of course the woods were full of rabbits, so they had some meat. Then, too, the cows still kept them supplied with milk, butter, and cream. The hens quit laying during the middle of the winter but would resume their duties again as soon as the spring thaw began.

There was a happy reunion in the spring when the men returned from Hibbing. Excitedly the children surrounded them. Krist and Helmer were eager to tell them about the store having burned down. It surprised them that the men already knew about it. Everyone was then thrilled to see that the men had loaded their pack sacks with the staples most needed and appreciated, flour, coffee, and sugar. By Easter the hens were laying again. There were enough eggs for everyone to have two or three, with freshly baked bread, both of which were doubly relished because there had been a scarcity of them all winter.

## Chapter 5
## PIONEERS ON A HARSH FRONTIER

More and more families were homesteading in the North. Some from Finland had settled closer to the Norwegian-Swedish group. Most of them could speak a dialect called Swede-Finn. It was actually Swedish which had a unique lilt to it – as indeed all the Norwegian or Swedish dialects had, since each secluded district had its own peculiar variation of the national language. The Russian and Polish settlement five miles to the west had been growing rapidly since the first three immigrants had stayed at the cabin that rainy spring night. They were developing a large farm and were in desperate need of a market for their produce. The number of milk cows at the Skoglie / Persson homesteads gradually increased, but they, too, had no market for their cream and butter.

In 1909, Sanna gave birth to another daughter, but something was wrong and the infant only lived a short time after her birth. Sanna and Hans grieved, but the Lord comforted them, as they comforted each other. They were grateful for a loving family. Life goes on, and with time the pain subsided. [Our mother told us about it many years later and said that they buried the baby in the meadow. We picked bouquets of fragrant purple violets every May in that meadow, and we wondered where the little grave would be, or what our sister would have been like if she had lived.]

The Skoglies rejoiced when Sanna was again "in the family way," and Ellen Henrietta was born on May 27, 1910. Auntie Sarah naturally helped with the delivery. She herself had given birth to their ninth child, Bertha, about four months earlier, in January. Eventually Sarah was on call to deliver the new arrivals all over the growing community, as she would become known as the midwife to many homesteaders in the North Woods. She was capable, experienced, and willing to help. All women for miles around knew that she would come any time, day or night. Since there were no telephones in the early days

PHOTO 1908: Children of Andrew and Sarah Persson on the adjacent homestead. Back row: Helmer, Christina, and Anna. Front row: Albert, Arvid, Carl, and Sally. (The family eventually had eleven children. The three not yet born were Bertha, Hilding, and Elva.)

someone had to be sent to tell her it was time. Sometimes a boy would come running down the birch-lined lane to the Perssons' homestead. Aunt Sarah would walk the two or three miles as fast as the boy could walk. We did not hear of her ever getting paid for her services except for an occasional piece of dress goods, some garden produce, or some other gift of gratitude, but she was not expecting any pay. She was often heard to say, *"Vi må være taksom for det lille vi få."* (We must be thankful for the little we get.) She considered it an honor to help others, and took great pride and delight in ushering new life into the homes of these fellow pioneers.

Sanna was happy to have Sarah nearby, not only for the security of having a midwife for the birth of her children, but because they enjoyed a close friendship. Andrew, didn't mind taking care of things at home when Sarah was elsewhere delivering a baby, or was just having some time at the Skoglies for a chat with Sanna.

During that same summer, a diphtheria epidemic broke

PHOTO 1908: The Persson Clan. Back Row: Helmer Persson, Anders Persson (holding Carl "Calleh"), Sarah Persson, Jonas "Krist," Christina Persson, Sanna and Hans Skoglie (holding Johnny). Front Row: Albert, Arvid, and Anna Persson, Grandpa Jonas and Grandma Kristina, Girls in Front: Sally Persson and Laura Skoglie.

out in the community. The pioneers did not run to a doctor for every little ache or pain. Some of them never saw a doctor or the inside of a hospital. In those days it took the better part of a day to go by horseback the twenty-five miles to the nearest town of Cook to fetch a doctor, and another day to return. Many times, when the doctor arrived, the ailing one had already passed away.

It is not known how far the epidemic had spread, but most of the children in the area had the illness to some degree. Laura had a mild case. Johnny was so sick that he was close to death. Thankfully baby Ellen was not sick at all. Since she was being breast fed, no doubt she had built up immunities.

The Gust Hill family, Swede-Finns who were our closest neighbors to the east, were hit the hardest. They had six children, the three youngest being about the same ages as Laura, Johnny and Ellen. Several of their children were very ill. By the time the doctor got there, their three eldest children, two girls and a boy, had already succumbed to the dread disease. Another little boy had just become ill. With proper medication given in time, the doctor was able to save that little one's life.

Since diphtheria was so contagious, no one could visit their neighbors, nor attend a funeral. Anyone who lost a family member had to dig the grave and bury his own loved one. With his eyes brimming with tears, Gust Hill said that he had never lifted anything as heavy as the shovels full of dirt with which he buried his three dead children!

In September of 1910, Hans was working in a swamp. He had found some rich black soil there and thought that if he could drain it, it might be a wonderful place to grow vegetables the following year. He was digging ditches to drain off the water. One day late in the month, he forgot to bring drinking water with him, so he dipped water out of the ditch and drank that. When he became ill, Sanna thought he had contracted diphtheria, but it puzzled her that the symptoms were different. Aunt Sarah came to try to help suggest remedies, but only shook her head in dismay as the illness grew progressively worse. It is not known how long he was sick at home before he was taken by horse and wagon to Grand Rapids. Hibbing, only forty miles away, had doctors and a hospital, but since the Skoglies had little money and no insurance, he had to be taken to the county hospital which was in Grand Rapids, the county seat. The trip was thirty miles farther than Hibbing.

Over a month later, Sanna knew there was bad news when she saw her mother coming slowly across the clearing with head down and her hands clasped behind her back. The postmaster from Celina had brought a letter addressed to Mrs. Hans Skoglie. The envelope was edged in black, indicating it was a death notice. It was postmarked from Grand Rapids. It informed her that Hans at age 36, had died of typhoid fever and had been buried there.

Sanna felt as though her world had come to an end. She did not know how she could face life from day to day without her beloved Hans. She lay awake nights, unable to sleep, and her pillow was soaked with her tears. She knew life must go on, and that somehow, she must raise the children. She tried to stay strong, not weeping in front of them. It was so hard to answer the children's searching questions or to know how to comfort them, while she herself was crushed with grief.

Each day, the 27-year-old widow wrote in a small journal which she kept tucked away in an old blue trunk Hans had brought from Norway. In her writings, she poured out her heartfelt agony, expressing the deep sorrow at the loss of her Hans. It told mostly of her loneliness, and how much she missed him, and how dear little Johnny cried for his papa. She also wrote that perhaps the baby was lucky because she couldn't remember him. [That baby was Ellen who years later found the diary and read it. She understood it better than the younger children, because she could read Swedish. Ellen said, "Of course, I was too young to remember him, but it is a strange and sad feeling never to have seen or known the face of your own father. I know only what my mother told me of their life together, and of her sad and lonely time after he was gone."]

An excerpt from that journal reads: "Death has wrenched my husband from my side. Yes, he is gone, gone forever. By God's mercy he no longer has to struggle with poverty, sickness, and dashed hopes here in this dark world. He never complained. He always thanked God for his family and many times prayed that God would bless and keep us, his dearest in the world. My thoughts question, 'Why did God take him away?' But I know it is His will. God sees the depths of my sorrow. I shall never forget my beloved Hans, but with You, my God, I shall meet him again."

Sanna kept busy, trying to fill the great void in her life with raising her three children. She did not mind the barn chores or the numerous household tasks. She knew that life would have been meaningless if she didn't have the children. She had no appetite and noticed that her clothes hung loosely on her. She was getting thinner each day, but did not care. She worried about keeping the little ones fed. She had potatoes, rutabagas and carrots from their garden. There were a few eggs, but she knew that the chickens would quit laying entirely when the bitter cold of winter would come. There was still some milk from one of the cows, but that would go dry soon for her calving time. She snared rabbits to add meat to their diet, yet she did not know what she would do when her supply of rice, flour, oatmeal and sugar would be gone. She kept reminding herself not to worry but to put her trust in God. Surely, He would provide for their needs, as it says in Psalm 146:9b *"...He relieveth the fatherless and widow..."*

Each Sunday the three families were accustomed to meeting for worship. Usually they met in Sanna's home, but occasionally they met at Jonas' or at Andrew's place. Sanna welcomed the Lord's Day - a time to take her focus off of her loss and to praise God by considering that Hans was in the very presence of Jesus.

A Swedish Covenant pastor, who farmed near Celina, walked to surrounding communities to conduct Sunday "Meetings." He did not come to their homesteads very often - only a few Sundays during the spring, summer or fall months. Other

PHOTO: Church Meeting at Sanna's. Sanna is by the corner of the house, with Ellen in front of her. They are standing next to Sanna's father, Jonas, and her brother, Andrew. Johnny is in front of them. Daughter Laura has hands together and her head cocked to one side. Grandma Kristina is by the window, dressed in black with Sarah behind her.

neighbors joined them when the pastor was there, but generally it was only the members of the three households.

Sanna's father, "Grandpa Jonas" taught a Sunday School class for all his grandchildren. He had blue eyes, a bushy beard,

31

PHOTO: Grandpa Jonas' Sunday School Class. Front: Ellen seated by "Grandpa." Back row: Johnny, Laura, and cousins Anna, Albert and Sally

and a soft heart. He was known for being a God-fearing man, and the children loved him. Jonas was 62 years old when Hans died. All the relatives nearby were a great help and comfort to Sanna. She was grateful for all that they did for her and the children. Her parents were in good health and came often, but she did not want them to come when the weather became bitterly cold for fear they would become ill. Her brother, Krist, had obtained a rifle, so occasionally he brought a partridge or some venison. Andrew and Sarah would come as often as they could, even though they had their own large family to care for. They always brought gifts of food. Sarah chatted with Sanna over coffee while Andrew chopped and carried in stacks of wood. Sarah was a great comfort to Sanna in

PHOTO: Krist and Helmer out hunting

the time of her bereavement.

Early in 1911, Sanna's father felt it was time to proof their homesteads so that the land could be legally theirs. The Homestead Act required at least five years of continual occupancy before the "final proof" could be made. By now, they had lived on their properties nearly six years. Since it was 1907 before Andrew made the initial filing for his homestead, his could not be completed yet. However, the "Jonasson" homestead (as Jonas and Kristina's place was called) as well as Hans and Sanna Skoglie's claim, could be finalized. The previous spring, William Halbesleben, a neighbor to the east, had completed the paperwork for his homestead, so he had described to Jonas what all needed to be done.

Early in the morning of February 8th, Sanna left her children with her mother. Krist hitched the horses to a sleigh, then drove his father and sister to Cook where the two of them boarded a train to Duluth. Sanna stared out the window at the snow-covered landscape - her heart heavy. She didn't relish having to do this legal work. If Hans were alive, he would have gladly made the trip. Lifting her eyes to the leaden skies, she quietly offered a simple prayer, "Lord, please help me to do this for Hans' sake, and for the children."

Just then, her father put his hand on hers, giving it a bit of a squeeze. He spoke gently, "God will help us through this."

She had to smile as she turned and looked into his loving eyes. She sighed, "Yes Pa, thanks. I needed that reminder."

The following day, Thursday, February 9, Jonas and Sanna went to the United States Land Office where they signed papers to declare their intention to finalize their claims. They had to name four people, two of which could later serve as witnesses. They also gave the name of the nearest newspaper for their area, which was the *Bear River*, a weekly journal.

This was only the beginning in the process for establishing claim to their homesteads. The man at the land office told them what would take place next. Two news articles – one about Jonas, and the other about Sanna - would be sent to the *Bear River* paper. Sanna's read, "Dept. of the Interior, U.S. Land Office at Duluth, Minn, Feb. 9, 1911. Notice is hereby given that Elise Skoglie of Celina, Minn, who on August 15, 1904, made homestead entry for NE quarter, section 11, Township 62N, Range 22W, 4th Principle Meridian, has filed notice of intention to make final five year proof to establish claim to the land above described." The notices would be run in the paper for five consecutive weeks, probably for the purpose of seeing if anyone would come forward and object to the right to their claims. Then, the filling out of forms for the final "proof," needed to be made in Grand Rapids, the county seat for Itasca County, at which time, their witnesses would have to appear with them. A date was set for March 30.

Near the end of March, Jonas, Sanna, Andrew and a neighbor, Askar Karlsen, all went to Grand Rapids, 70 miles to the southwest. On March 28, Jonas, Andrew and Sanna each received their naturalization papers. [All immigrants had to take naturalization classes. These were offered in the one-room schools.] On March 30, 1911, both Jonas and Sanna filled out the final proof papers for their homesteads. The claimant had several pages of questions to answer – some of which included:

1. Name, age, address
2. Are you a native born citizen of the U.S? (If foreign-born, proof of naturalization had to be shown.)
3. Are you the same person who made homestead entry on August 15, 1904? (In Sanna's case, she had to explain that she was the widow of Hans Skoglie who made said entry.)
4. Married - Single – If married, list family members.
5. When did you first establish actual residence upon the land? When was your house built? Have you or your family ever been absent from the homestead? If so, give the dates and reason for each absence. (Sanna explained Hans' absence in winter months to earn money to support the family.)
6. Describe the land: How much cleared – cultivated – timbered? (Nine acres cleared and ready to cultivate. Five acres under cultivation. Planted and harvested crop

each year.)

7. Describe in detail any improvements made, and their value. (Sanna listed a 15 x 20 foot home with one door and two windows, an 18 x 20 foot barn, a root house, three wells, a chicken house, hay barn, and a wood shed, valued at a total of $700 dollars.)

8. Have you sold, or agreed to sell any portion of this land?

Each of the witnesses - Askar being one of them - had less questions to answer, but had to establish how long he had known the claimant, and how often he would see them. He also had to describe the improvements made to the homestead. Each of the answers were compared by officials. Papers then were sent to Duluth where they were stamped by the land office in April. Jonas and his daughter, Sanna, finally received their land patents in July. Sanna looked over the paperwork. She read, "...the claim of Elise Skoglie, widow of Hans M. Skoglie, has been established and duly consummated, in conformity to the law...28th day of July, 1911." - Signed by President William H. Taft. It was bittersweet to now own the land - but, oh, if only Hans could have seen this day! He had worked so hard to fulfill this dream. She had to remind herself that he was in a much better place - his true home in heaven. Jesus had promised, "...*I go to prepare a place for you.*" (John 14:2)

Andrew and Sarah Persson did the final proof for their homestead in the summer of 1913, and received the patent for their land in January of 1914.

\* \* \* \*

After a few months, Sanna began having visitors. There were several lonely bachelors who came at different times to call on the pretty young widow. At that time, she had no interest in any of them. She cared least of all for one who succeeded in making a real nuisance of himself. When she awakened early one dark morning to the sound of his chopping wood by lantern light, her temper flared up and she told him in no uncertain terms to leave and never come back. Much to her relief, he took her advice and never bothered her again.

Later, she did become interested in one of the other callers. His name was John Gilbertson. Like Sanna's late husband, Hans, John, too, was an immigrant from Norway.

PHOTO: Sanna's children, Laura, Ellen, Johnny.

Chapter 6
TAMING THE WILDERNESS
by Helga

PHOTO: The town of Nes in Ådalen Valley of Buskerud County, Norway.

John Gilbertson was born August 17, 1880, at a place called Briskoden near Nes, in Buskerud County, Norway. This area was about 60 miles northwest of Oslo. By the time John was in his teens, many in this region were leaving to homestead in America. Some may wonder why. Norway is a beautiful country with mountains and a long rugged coastline, but much of it, because of its rugged terrain is not flat enough to cultivate. Only 3% of the land is farmable. People who lived near the coast were generally involved in the fishing industry. Those who lived inland had small farms and supplemented their livelihood by doing some logging. These farms would pass on to the eldest son in the family. It was no wonder that the news of free land in America was a strong lure for many. John's parents, as well as his grandparents, were all joining the throngs of immigrants.

John's mother, Kari, came from a large family. She was the second of nine children. Kari was already married when her parents, John and Inger Simonson, and some of her siblings immigrated to America. Some of those who had left as early as

# Helga's Great Grandparents

PHOTO: John and Inger Simonson, parents of Kari,
(Kari was John Gilbertson's mother)
The Simonson family was the first of my ancestors
to immigrate to America.

1885, were the first of my ancestors to immigrate. John Simonson was from Nes in Buskerud County, and his wife Inger's lineage had originated northwest of there, in the Valdres region of Oppland County. Kari and all of her siblings eventually left Norway. Six of the Simonson offspring settled in northern Wisconsin, two went to North Dakota. Kari would be the only one of the nine who eventually would move to Minnesota.

PHOTO: 1904 Kari and Gulbrand Johnson

Kari, with her husband, Gulbrand Johnson, and their four children: sons, John, 18, Johan, 13, and Helge, 10, and daughter, Inger, 6, left their homeland in 1898. They first journeyed down the inland fjord by boat to Oslo, then a day-and-a-half's journey across the North Sea to the east coast of England. By train they crossed to Liverpool where they secured passage on a larger ship which would take them to America. The three sons had had the surname of Gulbrandson because of being Gulbrand's sons, but after arriving in the New World, they Americanized it to Gilbertson.

When their ship passed by the Statue of Liberty and docked in New York, the passengers were ushered inside the immigration buildings on Ellis Island. Immigrants from nearly every European country were there. It must have sounded like it did at the Tower of Babel after God had confounded their language! At one point, while

PHOTO: John Gilbertson at age 18 in 1898, the year he came to America.

# Helga's Grandparents

PHOTO c. 1900: Parents of John Gilbertson: Gulbrand & Kari Johnson with their youngest son Helge.

they were waiting, Kari with some of the other Norwegian ladies, searched for a restroom. Seeing a door labeled PRIVATE, they promptly barged in, only to find a man seated at a desk. They turned quickly and went out again. They reasoned among themselves, "Did the word not mean the same as it does in the old country?!" (There, public restrooms would be labeled PRIVATE.)

It took some time to get everyone's papers processed. It took so long, in fact, that it was customary for the immigrants to be given some foods to snack on while waiting. An orange was among the snacks. Never having seen an orange before, one of the men bit into it, presuming it to be like an apple. Then he made a wry face and spat it out. Later they learned that they should have peeled it first. At last their paper work was completed. Gulbrand and Kari, with their three sons and little daughter, moved with the crowd to get to the railway station. Many of the immigrants, like themselves, were farmers who eagerly came to settle the free land given by the government.

They first went by train to northern Wisconsin where Kari's family had a home for them in the Hatley-Norrie area just east of Wausau. They farmed there for six years. It was there in Wisconsin that their little daughter, Inger, took sick and died.

By this time, Gulbrand's parents, John and Helga Anderson, and his two brothers, Anders and Erik, had immigrated. Gulbrand decided to join them, so in the spring of 1904, they packed up their belongings into their wagon, and hitched up their team of horses to move westward into Minnesota.

They signed up for a homestead and were granted a 160 acre quarter section in St. Louis County, west of Cook – about 80 miles northwest of Duluth.

PHOTO: John and Helga Anderson, paternal grandparents of John Gilbertson.

They would all work together to develop their homestead property. Building a homestead took much hard labor, yet since they had seven men to do the work, they had it easier than the Persson, Skoglie clan. They also had a team of horses to help in hauling timber or clearing land.

PHOTO: Cutting and hauling timber for building cabins

They pitched a big tent in which they could live and also store their supplies while they labored. They needed to cut timber for building cabins and a barn. Stumps had to be grubbed out and brush cut away to clear land for planting a vegetable garden and for growing hay to put up for winter feed for their cows and horses.

The three women, Helga Anderson and her two daughters-in-law, the wife of Anders and of Gulbrand, did the cooking and helped to prepare a garden. They had brought cured hams and bacon - meats that would need no refrigeration. They also picked wild strawberries, blueberries, raspberries, pin cherries, and June berries which were found in abundance, canning them for winter use. By autumn, they had built two log cabins: one for Gulbrand and Kari's family with their three sons, the other for Gulbrand's parents and his two brothers. They also had made a corral and a small barn for their horses.

By the time winter's arctic temperatures were upon them, their first crop of potatoes, carrots and rutabagas were stored away. Their most staple meats were rabbit, fish, and venison. In those early years there were no game wardens, nor were there any laws against hunting in any season. That was a good thing since the immigrants depended on the wild game for their daily food. Occasionally they shot a moose or a bear. If they got big game in summer, they canned the meat or shared it with friends and neighbors. In winter it was no problem to keep meat frozen, but it had to be stored in a secure place to keep wolves or Canadian lynx from getting it.

PHOTO: May 17, 1904 Norway's Independence Day. They are flying the Norwegian flag.

PHOTO: While building cabins on the homestead, they stayed in a tent. Left to Right: Gulbrand and Kari Johnson, Gulbrand's parents, John and Helga Anderson, Anders with his wife, then Helge, Erik, and Johan. (John Gilbertson took the photo 1904)

PHOTO 1904: Helge and Johan, Anders, John and Helga Anderson, Kari and Gulbrand Johnson

PHOTO: Johnson farm 1904. A home for Gulbrand's parents and brothers. Left to Right: John and Helga Anderson (Gulbrand's parents) Anders (Gulbrand's brother) Johan and Helge (Gulbrand's sons) Kari and Gulbrand Johnson (Parents of John Gilbertson). parents) Anders (Gulbrand's brother) Johan and Helge (Gulbrand's sons) Kari and Gulbrand Johnson (Parents of John Gilbertson).

PHOTO 1905: Gulbrand and Kari Johnson's Homestead.

Gulbrand, Kari and their sons managed through the first winter in their small cabin, but in the summer of 1905 they added a bedroom, and also built a roofed porch at the front entrance. They increased the height of the stove pipe considerably. [They must have had problems with it smoking into the cabin.]

PHOTO: John Gilbertson's Homestead in Linden Grove near Cook, Minnesota.

John was age twenty-three when the family moved from Wisconsin to Minnesota. He personally filed for another homestead and got one in Linden Grove, just seven miles west of Cook. He built a small cabin on his place.

He then became the postmaster for Celina, making the tough twenty-two mile trips back and forth from Cook to get the mail. It was through his work as a mailman that he met the young widow, Sanna Elise Skoglie.

## Chapter 7
## SANNA MARRIES AGAIN

Since John Gilbertson was the postmaster for the Celina region, it was he who had brought the black-edged letter to Sanna's parents, containing the crushing news of Hans' death. As previously mentioned, local bachelors called on Sanna, but she neither encouraged nor welcomed them. Then, when John, out of concern, occasionally dropped in to check on the widow, she took an interest in him.

PHOTO: John visited Mrs. Skoglie and took this photo of her with her children and some of her brother Andrew's family. Left to right: Helmer and Anna Persson, Laura, Sanna holding Ellen, Johnny in front of her, Sally, Arvid, and Albert Persson. At far right Sanna's brothers, Krist and Andrew.

John took this photo November 26, 1911, when he was checking on Sanna. The same day he also took a picture of her brother Andrew's place. Then he sent the photos to them on penny postcards, postmarked Dec 12. Written on the back of each was the simple message, *"Venlig Hilsen fra* (friendly greetings from) John Gilbertson."

PHOTO Nov 26, 1911: John Gilbertson visited the Andrew Persson homestead.

When John first came to visit, the children were shy and fearful - as they were of all strangers. Laura and Johnny ran and hid. Ellen clung to her mother. The next time he came, he brought his fiddle and played for them. Sanna appreciated hearing many old favorites. As John swung into the lively strains of "The Irish Washer Woman" and *"Johan på Snippen,"* Laura and Johnny came out of hiding and stood wide-eyed, watching the musician.

PHOTO 1912: John Gilbertson with Sanna and children.
Standing: Sanna's brother Krist

# Helga's Parents

PHOTO: John and Sanna Gilbertson's wedding day, June 25, 1912. Sanna had borrowed the dress from her niece, Christina Persson.

After a year's courtship, John proposed to Sanna. On June 25th, 1912, he came and escorted her to Celina where they were married at the Swedish-Covenant pastor's home, the one who from time to time conducted meetings at the homestead.

PHOTO: June 25, 1912 WEDDING DAY John and Sanna with her children: Laura, Johnny, Ellen.

    John came to live on his wife's homestead with his newly acquired family. Sanna soon realized that John was not a farmer as Hans had been. John had no patience with animals and he seemed to make them nervous so they would kick or jump about. Sanna didn't mind doing the chores if John would just stay out of the barn. In Sweden it was customary for the women to do the milking anyway.
    John was talented in many other areas - a jack of all trades. He was a good blacksmith, and excelled in anything mechanical. He liked to repair all makes of clocks and watches. In later years, he bought a shoemaker machine so he could half-sole shoes, sew torn seams, or put on new rubber heels. He also was a musician and had even made a violin.

PHOTO: 1913 The homestead where John and Sanna Gilbertson and their family lived.

PHOTO: 1913 Gilbertson Pioneer Family.
Left to Right: Johnny, 5, John holding Ellen, 3, Sanna, and Laura, 8.

Photography was another of John's many interests. He owned a big professional camera. Negatives were on glass in those days and John scratched his name, or initials and dates on them. Most of the older pictures in this book were taken by him. When he wanted to take a picture, he would set up the camera on a tripod. He would drape a black cloth over his head as he got the picture in focus, then he would stick his head out and make sure no one moved before he pressed the bulb. He had a backdrop that must have been very expensive for those days. It had a lovely curving staircase with some big urns of beautiful flowers on it. Sometimes Sanna was a bit perturbed when John would announce that they should assemble for a portrait. She said, "He would come rushing in, full of enthusiasm, and because he felt like taking our picture, he thought that I should be excited about it too." Years later, she laughed about some of those spur of the moment portraits. In one, Sanna doesn't look too happy about the whole thing. She was wearing her usual house dress and was "in the family way." John had tattered work pants, Laura and Johnny wore the old clothes they used when piling wood, and Ellen had a shapeless, homemade dress, sagging stockings, and a pouting expression. At least Ellen and Laura's hair was nicely braided. Sanna was never too busy to comb and braid their hair every morning.

On August 4, 1913, Karl Gunhard, John's first child, was added to the family. At the time, Ellen was age 3. Although she was so young, Ellen recalls, "I do remember that morning of August 4 when my stepfather carried me into my mother's bedroom, which was actually only a partitioned off corner of the kitchen, and showed me a fuzzy little head sticking out of the blanket beside my mother. I was not especially interested in the little imposter, and I could not understand how he had appeared on the scene so suddenly – nor why. We had been a perfectly complete family without him. I puzzled over it for days and asked my older sister, who was then eight years old, but she only laughed at me. My mother did say that I became devoted to him within a few weeks."

# Chapter 8
## NASS STORE AND POST OFFICE
### by Ellen

PHOTO: School Picnic at M. Hall - 1909

More immigrants were moving into the area. With long winters which kept people indoors, our socializing was done in summertime. We would have a gathering of neighbors for a meal such as on July 4th, or following a church service at one of our homesteads. At other times, neighbors helped one another build a barn, or make "shakes," (cedar shake shingles for a roof.) Since homes were small, generally a long crude table and benches were constructed outside for the mealtime.

PHOTO: Picnic at Amunson's, June 29, 1913

PHOTO: Picnic at Axel Mattson's, June 14, 1913. At left, Andrew and Sarah Persson with four of their children, then Johnny, Sanna and Ellen. Laura is at the far right in white.

During 1913 and 1914, there was a lot of activity on the homestead. Two long log additions were added to the cabin. The west wing was erected first. It became our living room/bedroom, with one corner partitioned off for the new post office. Pa's duties as postmaster legally transfered from Celina to this new location in 1913. Since Pa was from Nes in Norway ("Nes" means a nose-like peninsula), and Ma spoke of Naset, "the peninsula" where her family had lived in Sweden, they agreed upon the name – Nass Post Office. Although Pa was the postmaster, Ma's bachelor brother, our "Uncle Krist," took on the responsibility of being the first mail carrier for Nass. By the time Nass Post Office officially opened, he was under contract to make the mail runs from Cook.

Roads were rutted and muddy making the trip difficult. Before there were any cars in the region, he used horses and a wagon in summer, and hitched the team to a long sleigh in winter. For the cold season, Krist grew a beard for warmth. When temperatures plunged well below zero, he wore a knee-length sheepskin-lined coat. At times he had to run behind the sleigh to keep from freezing. Winter's darkness set in by 4 o'clock, yet Uncle Krist would not arrive home until 7 o'clock. By then he had icicles in his beard. On Mondays, Wednesdays and Fridays he picked up the outgoing mail and traveled the twenty-five miles to Cook. He made the return trip on the alternate days: Tuesdays, Thursdays and Saturdays.

The post office used a corner of the living room only that first year. In 1914, a wider addition was added on the south side of the cabin. Many homesteads in the North Woods were far from any town, so Pa had determined to build this big addition to become a store as well as the post office. By springtime, the construction of the store was well underway when Inger Josie was born on May 9, 1915. Our mother had been ailing all that winter, and was very thin. After the birth, Ma was taken by wagon to Cook, then by train the additional 70 miles to Duluth to have gallbladder surgery.

PHOTO: Krist Persson
Mail Carrier for Nass

Our cousin Anna was called upon to help out, but since she was only fourteen, there would be too much responsibility for her to stay a long time. So Pa brought home an elderly Norwegian lady from Cook to look after the five of us while Ma was away. The lady was probably about forty-five, but of course, that seemed old to us. We thought it took her forever to get a meal on the table, but there was a tiny infant, Inger, and two-year-old Karl to take care of, as well as all the housework to do.

Laura, who was nearly ten years old, was probably a good

PHOTO 1915: Nass Store and Post Office. Left to Right: Johnny, Ellen, Sanna holding Inger, Laura, and John holding Karl

PHOTO 1916: A Sunday gathering beside the store. **The Gilbertsons** (lower right): Sanna seated with Inger 1, on her lap. At far right, Laura 11, and Johnny 8. Karl 3, and Ellen 6, left of Sanna. **The Perssons:** Row 1: Elva 1, Grandma Kristina in black, Hilding 4, and Bertha 6. Row 2: Sarah seated, Sally 10, Carl 9. Row 3: Arvid 12, a friend, Anna 16, a friend, and Christina 23. Row 4: Albert 14, Helmer 20, and Andrew help, but Johnny and I made nuisances of ourselves. We would run in and out, holding the screen door open and letting flies in – not intentionally, but as all children do. Teasing our little brother Karl, however, was intentional! His little potty chair was set out in the entry during the day. We thought it was great fun to dip the willow whisk in water and swish it over him. When he set up a howl of protest, we would run out and hide. We were sure the lady would tell Pa about it, but still we persisted in tormenting our poor little brother. I don't recall what the consequences were. Very likely Johnny received the punishment because he was older and Pa said, "He should have known better." At the time, Johnny was eight and I was only five, so it might have been true, but I heard that remark so often, I became confident I would not be punished. I planned many of the escapades that were perpetrated by the two of us, and he got punished for them. I never denied being the instigator, but then, nobody asked me either! They took it for granted that I was too young to think of so many naughty tricks.

The store was completed that summer of 1915. The main door was on the south end, flanked by large double windows. Extending back along the west side was the post office area with a tall section of lock boxes as well as call boxes separating the office area and the patrons' waiting room in the center of that part of the building.

On the east wall were shelves that reached to the ceiling with a high counter separating the patrons and customers from the merchandise. It was necessary to keep the little gate hooked from the owner's side. There were only a very few who were not to be trusted, but our parents could not afford to lose even a few cents through petty shoplifting. A bell on the door at the business end alerted us whenever a customer entered. We also had a window in the door that separated the store from the kitchen.

My parents ordered any needed hardware items from

Marshall Wells, and other supplies, especially groceries, but also some dry-goods from Stone, Ordean Wells, Co. Both companies were in Duluth. Everything arrived by mail to Cook. After Uncle Krist loaded it all in town, he would deliver the mail and supplies to the three post offices along his route. Meadowbrook, the first post office out from Cook, handled only postal service. Celina had a small store, so he hauled groceries and other supplies that had been ordered for both Celina and Nass. Sometimes it was a lot to deliver.

One day Ma sold a shirt to a Polish man. After about a week, he returned saying the shirt was too small. When Ma saw the double rings of sweat around the collar as well as the cuffs, she said, "You can't return this. It's been worn until it is dirty."

The man admitted to wearing it to a wedding. We knew that the Polish weddings lasted three days and three nights.

One afternoon Nels Nelson and his young son entered the store. When Nels spotted the jar of candy on the counter, he turned to the boy and asked, "Do you want some candy, Arthur?" Evidently having second thoughts about having to part with a penny, Nels quickly added, "Nah!" Then he turned to look for the items he had come to buy.

Ma, seeing the disappointment on the boy's face, reached into the candy jar and found some broken pieces to slip to little Arthur. She was rewarded by seeing his sad countenance lift into a sweet smile. "*Tusen Takk* (Thank you)," he whispered.

I suppose the shelves in the store were not very fully stocked at first, but I recall some of the products that were sold in that early general store. There were some canned goods which had to be hauled in before winter or they would have been frozen solid on the long drive. The most dependable meat products were salt pork, bacon, and summer sausage. I was fascinated by the Gold Dust Twins on the package of soap powder. I also enjoyed staring at the picture within a picture on the Uzar Peanut Butter. On the label was a woman holding a jar of Uzar, on which was a smaller woman holding a jar, on which was a smaller woman ... I wondered how far the illustration went and how tiny the illustration would become, or would it go on and on? Three brands of coffee I can recall were the Arbuckle Brand, the XXXX, or 4X, but the customers always asked for the "XXXX." It was very good coffee, and not "Brand X." For really special occasions, however, our mother used the "steel ground" Empress Coffee. The other two brands came as whole coffee beans and were ground as needed with a coffee grinder.

We all drank coffee. Pa said that it was good for us and would give us a lot of pep and energy. Ma wasn't quite so sure it was good for us, especially since I stayed so skinny. When we did drink milk, it was skim milk. I liked to scoop off the foam after it poured out of the cream separator, and drink or eat that. By the time I was school age I would also head for the coffee pot when I came home from school. I would pour myself a big cupful and stir in two or three teaspoonfuls of sugar. With the foam and the sweet coffee, I probably was seldom hungry.

Pa also thought that mush was a good substantial supper for us. My digestion rebelled at the thought of it. I seldom ate more then a few spoonfuls, so, one evening he was determined that I should sit there until I finished my big wide soup-bowlful. I choked it down and then it all came back up into the bowl. It must have been an unappetizing scene! At least Pa never forced me to eat more than I wanted of it after that!

My conscience began to punish me that very year. Pa had been trying to instill the fear of God into us, and he succeeded with me, at least. He told us, "Unless you are good, you won't get to heaven, because God doesn't want sinners in heaven." I had told lies. I had stolen goodies from the pantry and from the store. Thou shalt not lie. Thou shalt not steal. Those were the two commandments I knew I had broken. I concluded I was definitely a sinner. God did not want sinners in heaven, so I knew there was no hope for me. I was bound for hell.

From then on, this awful and hopeless conviction hung over me like a cloud. Then, because I had a fear of dying, I became very cautious and fearful of anything that might bring about the end of my life. I had heard about mad dogs, so I became fearful of all dogs. We did not have a dog of our own at the time, but other customers would bring their dogs with them.

While the master waited for the mail to come, the dog would be snuffling around our yard. People came any hour of the day on any day of the week. If the business door was locked in the evening or on Sundays, the customer would come around to the kitchen door. The only way my parents could get away from the business was to lock up on Sundays and go to the Perssons' homestead where our weekly church services were then being held.

I recall one Sunday when there was a large dog in our yard, so I hid in the "little house," which is to say, the outhouse. The rest of the family, all dressed up and ready for the meeting at Uncle Andrew's home, were calling my name and looking for me. Since I could see through a crack that the dog had stationed himself right in front of the door of my odorous retreat, I dared not venture out, or even answer them. When they did find me, they scolded me for making us all late for the services.

About that time, around 1915, Pa's parents, Gulbrand and Kari Johnson, plus his brothers, Johan and Helge had plans of moving to Florida. Before leaving, they came to our home for dinner. I was five years old at the time. I was all dressed up in a white lace dress, and as I ran across the meadow to meet them, I forgot all about their big dog, Bamse. He ran ahead of them - to greet me I suppose - but I ran screaming back to the house and dived under Ma's bed. Then Bamse, still set on giving me a proper greeting, crawled under the bed after me. I probably beat the world record for getting out from under the bed. They put the dog outside, but my day had already been ruined and so was my nice white dress.

PHOTO: Helge and Johan

Later, while our grandparents and uncles were living in Florida, they sent us a big box of fruit. There were some regular sized sweet oranges, but there were also some enormous ones. They were such a pale yellow that they looked more like lemons. Pa said, "I've never seen such big oranges." After peeling one and popping a section of it into his mouth, he made a face and spit it out. "That is the sourest orange I ever tasted!" He exclaimed. That was our introduction to grapefruit. We all tried it, but couldn't eat it. Years later I learned to enjoy its tart taste.

In our home we had an Edison Victrola phonograph. Its long morning glory shaped horn was painted blue with deeper blue morning glories circling the fluted rim of the horn. It sat on top of the cabinet which could be pulled down to form a long, wide bed at night. The Victrola played single-song cylindrical recordings. We did not work on Sundays, it was the Lord's Day. So whenever Pa and Ma got some new recordings which they ordered through the mail, the entire clan would come over the following Sunday afternoon. Since by then we had already heard the recordings a few times, we would rather have been playing with our cousins than to have to sit quietly while some high-pitched female voice shrieked "Only a Flower from Home Sweet Home," or to hear McCormack thundering out one of his numbers. Admittedly I loved the instrumental pieces. I remember asking Ma to play some of them, especially "Over the Waves Waltz." I could listen to them by the hour, but each cylinder played only three minutes. If Ma was busy with her morning work, she barely had time to pick up the broom when she had to change the recording again. Also, she had to turn the crank on the side of the machine to wind up the spring. If she forgot to turn the crank until the spring was tight, it would run down and bellow like a sick cow as the speed decreased. At least that's what it sounded like to me. The first time that happened when I was in the room alone, it scared me nearly out of my wits. I ran screaming into the kitchen, "Ma, it's bellowing again!" Then, of course, that became a family saying. It seemed to me that I said a lot of dumb things that became family sayings, but then I suppose the other kids said some dumb things too.

\*   \*   \*   \*

Pa brought home a Ford touring car the summer of 1916. The arrival of that car was quite an event. All of us relatives were standing outdoors, watching for him to come from the town of Virginia. We were gathered in the narrow lane between the barbed wire fences of our pasture and of Uncle Andrew's, some distance from the house. There was no road because our home and store had been built in the middle of our homestead section. To get onto any road, we had to meander through the trees, down the lanes and through cattle gates. There was no road leading into our place from the east either, except a rough corduroy swamp road - that is where logs were laid parallel to fill in a swampy area.

Finally, we heard the chugging noise of the motor as the car came rumbling down from Grandfather's pasture. The rumbling, rattling and chugging noise increased in volume as it came closer. The strange contraption was upon us almost as soon as we heard the sound. We children stood staring wide-eyed, excited yet fearful, when the noisy buggy came weaving its way between the trees. I am certain that we stepped back and gave it plenty of room. It was the first car I had ever seen. My cousin, four-year-old Hilding said, *"Nå men! Der kommer vogn uten hesten!"* (Wow! There comes a wagon without the horse!)

I had always had such a dread of motors. When Ma would begin to turn the crank of the cream separator I would run out. Pa also had a tall gasoline motor out in the shed that he started by stepping down on one of the big wheels. If Johnny wanted me out of the shed, he would act like he was going to step down on one of those wheels. Later it occurred to me that he probably wasn't heavy or strong enough to start it anyway, but it had the desired affect of sending me scurrying back to the house. Now my heart raced to see this noisy car.

Pa was in his glory, grinning from ear to ear as he sat behind the steering wheel. He applied the brakes so the family could ride the remainder of the way to the house. Johnny, knowing about my fear of motors, had been teasing me, saying, "You might as well start walking home because you will never dare to ride in it anyway."

Inger, age one, in Ma's arms, had not stopped screaming from the moment she saw and heard the black monster that made such frightening noises. Ma held her close and shouted to Pa to shut off the motor, but he replied, "I can't, or I'll have to crank it again to get it started." Ma had to walk back to the house, still trying to quiet the screaming child in her arms.

I don't recall if Pa told us to get in or not, but I was the first one to climb into the back seat. I think I surprised myself by my own boldness. Was it because Johnny had teased me? He, Laura and Karl all scrambled in behind me. Pa turned around and stared at me sitting high up on the back seat. Then he shook his head in wonder and amazement. Here I was, at age six, the first one to climb up into this noisy thing called a car or automobile. We all enjoyed the adventure of the ride to the house. At last I had discovered a motor that was attractive and interesting in spite of its noise. After that I was never far away when Pa mentioned driving off somewhere in the Ford, and my begging and crying nearly always produced the desired results. I enjoyed the rides in the horseless carriage.

PHOTO: Grinding grain for cattle feed. Andrew and Sarah feed grain into the machine, powered by a large gas engine (behind Andrew.) Grandpa Jonas is using a homemade rake with wooden tines.

68

## Chapter 9
## THE GREAT WAR
### by Ellen

After Helga's birth on that snowy March morning in 1917, the weather became milder and the crows returned, announcing the arrival of spring with their raucous "Caw, caw, caw!" The warm sun made lakes and rivers out of the snow.

When the hot days of summer finally came, my sisters, brothers and I spent most of the daylight hours playing outside. Our delighted screams and laughter, and shouts in Norwegian or Swedish could be heard from inside the cabin.

\* \* \* \*

When Helga was nine months old, she was walking. I wonder if Ma ever forgave Pa for showing that toddler how to put her foot on a chair rung so she could get up on a chair! She climbed up on the table, onto beds, on top of anything that had room for a hand and a foot, whether or not it tipped over or she would take a bad fall. Ma knitted her a thick woolen cap that she wore every waking moment to protect her, as she feared Helga might puncture her skull if she were to come down head first onto a pine knot sticking up in the rough board floor.

\* \* \* \*

Life may have appeared tranquil and normal in the North Woods, but a cloud was looming on the horizon – a threat of war. Newspapers were full of the news, and America was gearing up to help its allies. We had two weekly papers and a daily paper. One weekly came from Cook, 25 miles east in St Louis County. The other weekly came from Grand Rapids, 70 miles at the opposite end of Itasca County. Our daily paper was the *Duluth Herald*. Since we did not have daily mail service, we would receive two papers on mail days, which were three days a week.

Helga, being a few months old, and Inger and Karl being younger than I, understood nothing of all the talk about "The Great War," as World War I was called at the time. When the rumblings of war drew closer through the newspapers and rumors, they disturbed the tranquility of our little community as much as in any other part of our country. The settlers west of us were concerned about relatives in Poland, Russia and Austria. Feelings ran high, and anyone who even made a statement that was interpreted as being pro-German was ostracized. Families who happened to be of German origin, even though perhaps not at all in sympathy with the Kaiser, nevertheless, were not considered as trustworthy American citizens. It was not strange the children who absorbed this atmosphere in their homes should take it upon themselves to torment the one family that was only part German. In school we would not let them play with us – the "holy" Swedes, Norwegians, and Americans.

I suppose our elders had swallowed some propaganda that spread along with the war news. However, there was one part of it that Pa would not accept - some were pushing to do away with all use of foreign languages, even in the homes. Pa was not opposed to learning English. That was necessary. It was the language of this new land. Yet he spoke good Oslo Norwegian. It was his heart language. He didn't want us to be ashamed of our mother tongue, so he insisted we speak it in the home. Well, our speech was not as pure Norwegian as Pa's, but we rather spoke a mixture of Swedish, and Norwegian. After all, our mother was a Swede, and so was her brother's family who lived near us. We were with our cousins a lot, and they spoke Swedish. In the process we were blessed to have learned not only both Norwegian and Swedish, but also the language of our adopted country.

Some leading officials and volunteers came around to the one room schools in the area to sell Liberty Stamps to help the war effort. I do not think any of the children in our school had any money to buy anything. Adults were also urged to buy Liberty Bonds. It's doubtful that the parents could afford those either. Another suggestion for helping the war effort was for each child to tend his own "Liberty Garden" – a little plot of ground that each child was supposed to work to help the home food supply, so more surplus food could be sent to the war-torn countries in Europe. We didn't know that later the gardens would be inspected. I recall how ashamed I was when a woman came to inspect our gardens. I wasn't a very ambitious little kid at age seven, and I had a lovely crop of weeds.

Flour was rationed. Each family was permitted to buy only so many pounds of white flour per month. There was a dark, coarse mixture called "substitute flour," and of course, ingredients were not listed back then. There were rumors of sabotage. Auntie whispered to our mother about the Germans putting ground glass and other lethal substances in the substitute flour. Rice flour was another available substitute. We had that for sale in the store, too, but we used it mostly ourselves. The rice flour was white, so a problem was that other kids began to make snide remarks about our white bread. "They use all the white flour for themselves." We tried to explain and Ma even asked the teacher to tell the children about the rice flour, but they didn't believe it. Sugar was very expensive. Our mother was heard to say, "When sugar gets up to ten dollars for a hundred pound sack, it is just too much!" When considering that could have been ten days wages, it does sound very high.

One good thing for our community was that people were in a position to make money from their farms during the war years. Before Pa bought the Ford, local farmers sent their butter and eggs out with the mail wagon. Krist would bring back cash for them from Cook. After getting the car, Pa and Ma willingly exchanged everyone's dairy products, for merchandise out of the store, or for cash. Then, Pa would haul the cream, butter, and eggs to the town of Virginia, which was at least ten miles farther than Hibbing, but had a good market for farm produce.

Farmers were exempt from being drafted into the army. I suppose our woodsy pastures and small fields and meadows were classified as farms. None of the young men in our area were drafted, but our cousin Helmer, age 22, enlisted. Helmer's sister Anna, age 18, was engaged at the time to Carl Nelson, age

PHOTO: Helmer Persson in uniform, by his sister, Anna.

23. He, too, enlisted. Anna would have loved to have seen Carl more before his scheduled departure. However, with little more than two weeks remaining, his mother's home burned down. Carl, who deeply loved his mother, worked day and night to build her a new cabin so she would have shelter through the coming winter. Then both Helmer and Carl went away to fight for their adopted country.

They both were shipped out to Europe, to fight in France. Carl Nelson was in the famous "Lost Battalion." They were cut off by the enemy. Those hardy Minnesota farm kids and tough kids from cities out east, became men as they held

PHOTO: Carl's mother, Maren Nelson, by her home.

the line against unbeatable odds. The Germans came at them with flame throwers. Carl was gassed and was blind for a while. The gas also caused one finger to become rigid. One time when he was running to flee from the Germans, Carl dived under a fence and his pack got stuck. He had to squirm out of it to free himself and get away. Later He would say, "Yup, probably my pack is still hanging on a fence in France." He did safely return to marry our cousin Anna.

Helmer also fought in France. His battalion, although greatly outnumbered, succeeded in keeping the enemy from reaching Paris.

PHOTO: Carl Nelson and Anna (Persson) Wedding photo

Aunt Sarah, came more frequently to get her mail, hoping for a letter from her son. When she received one, she would always open it immediately and read it there where our mother could also hear the news. Then for a long time there were no more letters. As weeks went by with no word, there was a lot of gloom and weeping whenever Sarah came. They feared that Helmer was either missing in action or had been killed.

Finally, a letter came. Helmer had always written in Swedish. This letter, too, was in Swedish, but written in a strange hand. It was from a Swedish nurse in a hospital in France, written as he dictated to her. It informed them that Helmer had been seriously wounded in action by flying shrapnel from exploding shells, and that he also had been gassed. Because of the nature of his injuries, he had been unable to write or even to dictate a letter any sooner. He was in that hospital for a long time. Sanna and Sarah both wept and lifted their aprons to wipe their tears. That letter was very brief. After a few weeks, Sarah received longer letters, so in time they learned the details.

    Helmer's battalion had been in the battle of Boleau Woods. At one point, their unit had been cut off from supplies, and they were getting very hungry. Helmer had volunteered to go with a group to sneak through the enemy lines to bring back food for the soldiers. They had to pass through an area which the Germans were shelling, but getting hit was a risk they had to take, as they had been hungry too long. Upon obtaining bread, they thrust the loaves through with a long stick that they carried over their shoulders, then stealthily headed back to their lines. When they reached an open space, they ran across it one at a time, but Helmer was hit when he was in the middle of the clearing. His comrades dragged him off the field.

    Helmer was taken to a stone building that was being used as a hospital and was laid on a pallet on the floor of a large room. At one point he asked a nurse to move him from the middle of the floor over into a corner. The floors were covered with the wounded, but the nurse fulfilled the wish of the young soldier and had him moved. Shortly afterward, the Germans bombed the hospital, reducing it to a heap of rubble. The supporting structure of the building must have protected Helmer, for he was one of only three or four who survived that catastrophe of war. Surely the Lord had put it in his mind to request being moved into a corner. Our families praised the Lord that Helmer's life was spared. The Great War ended, and Helmer was transported back to America, but he would remain in a Veteran's hospital for a few more months.

*   *   *   *

    On June 19, 1918, our sister, Agnes Victoria, made her appearance. (It seemed proper to give her the name of Victoria since the war had been won.) Later, when she and Helga were toddlers, Ma enjoyed dressing them alike. Since they were only fourteen months apart, many folk would ask if they were twins.

*   *   *   *

    Before Helmer would return to Minnesota, another killer,

an epidemic, would bring great sorrow to our little clan up north. In 1919 the Spanish flu epidemic swept through the northlands. Both Grandma and Grandpa Persson got the flu, and when it turned into pneumonia, they didn't last long. They both had been sturdy, strong people, so no one expected the illness to take them down so quickly. Grandpa had been bringing us milk every day because our cows all happened to be having a dry period. The last day that our family saw him, he had come to bring the milk. He was riding on the stoneboat, pulled by oxen. (A "stoneboat" was a low raft-like box that was made for hauling rocks and stones out of a field.) He said at that time, "I have a little cold."

Karl, nearly age 6, had made a small wreathe from some creeping moss we had found in the swamp. He placed that wreathe on the low stoneboat as a gift for his grandfather.

Jonas smiled through his white whiskers as he stepped onto the stoneboat. "Thank you, Karl," he said in a loving tone. Then he returned to his home.

The following day when Uncle Krist came home after the mail run, he discovered that both his parents were very sick. He ran down the lane to get Sarah. She applied heat and musterole but was unable to break up the congestion and fever. Of course, there was no electricity, so there were no heating pads. None of us had a hot water bottle either. When Johnny had been very sick during the winter, Aunt Sarah had advised that a plate be heated, wrapped in a towel, and placed on his chest. The sound of his heavy breathing could be heard from the farthest corner of the house. Laura, too, had suffered with such a high fever that she had fever blisters around her mouth.

Grandma Kristina died May 9th, and Grandpa Jonas died twenty-two hours later on the 10th. Their funeral was held in their own home.  Though the house was filled with mourning relatives, neighbors, and friends, it seemed hollow and empty. I thought it so strange to see them lying so still in long wooden boxes.  The funeral was conducted by the Lutheran priest, Reverend Fadum who came from Cook.

As many as had transportation went the three miles to Celina for the burial.  Our mother couldn't go, since she had three little ones to care for.  She held eleven-month-old Agnes in her arms as she stood by the window to watch the wagon with the two caskets go down the road.  A newspaper clipping would state, "The deceased were well advanced in years..."  Yes, Jonas was 70 and Kristina 72.  That was considered old back then, yet Sanna had never known either of her parents to spend one day sick in bed.  It was a shock to lose them both so suddenly. *"Whereas ye know not what shall be on the morrow. For what is your life? It is even a vapour, that appeareth for a little time, and then vanisheth away."* (James 4:14)  Tears trickled down her cheeks as she watched in her silent pain.  Helga, age two, clung to her mama's skirts.  Inger, age four, stood close on the other side of Ma.  Neither of them understood what was happening, yet they sensed the atmosphere of grief and felt the insecurity as they saw their mother's tears.

Death was no stranger to Sanna.  She had lost a sister back in Sweden.  She and Hans had lost their third baby whom they had buried in the meadow.  She remembered the pain of Hans' death, and she knew not where he was buried - somewhere near the distant town of Grand Rapids.  Now her parents, too, were gone.  Death was a tough reality to the pioneers. Family members had to build the coffins and dig the graves.  At least being springtime the ground was thawed enough to have the burial.  It was hard on families when someone would die in winter.  Then they would have to store the bodies in a woodshed until spring when the ground would thaw enough to dig the graves.  In her heart Sanna knew she would see each of them again, as they all knew and loved the Lord, but for now she was numb in her pain.

Pa drove us four older children to the cemetery.  The

Celina church had not yet been built, but some of the men had been cutting brush for the church yard. They had some brush piles burning that day so I remember the smoke stinging my eyes. The Carlsons, a family we knew from Virginia were standing near us. I noticed that their eight-year-old daughter was weeping. When our eyes met, Florence wiped her tears and stammered, "The smoke is hurting my eyes." Later I told Ma that I thought Florence was crying.

Ma sighed and said, "I suppose she was thinking about her older brother who died last winter when the flu was hitting all the towns." Florence had had time to learn that the death of a loved one meant she would never see him again. I was a year older than Florence, but I didn't realize that truth until I began to miss Grandpa's brief visits, or the special times of going to their home for one of Grandma's good dinners. I also had not learned yet, that though we would not see them again on earth, we could see them in Heaven. A double headstone still marks the final resting place for their bodies, but their spirits went to be with Jesus. *"... to be absent from the body, and to be present with the Lord."* (II Cor. 5:8)

My younger siblings would not remember their maternal grandparents, but I remembered them well. Grandma had thick black hair and snapping dark eyes. She seemed to read a child's mind and knew full well when they thought of some mischief because she would stop them with one look from those piercing eyes. Grandpa was a gentle, kind-hearted man. His clear blue eyes showed his love for the children. They both were God-fearing folk. The first eleven grandchildren who had been in his Sunday School class during those early years on the homestead would dearly miss him after he died.

Life went on after that. Uncle Krist continued to live in his parents' home. It must have been lonely and quiet for him, but he was gone a lot. He still hauled mail and supplies, keeping him away much of six days a week. Gradually the roads were improved, making his trips easier.

When Helmer returned home at last, there was great rejoicing. A social was held in his honor. The local newspaper printed this article: "A social dance will be held at the Woodman Hall Tuesday evening in honor of Helmer Persson, one of our soldiers who has recently returned from France. Helmer was wounded twice during the battle of Boleau Woods, and has been in the hospital most of the time since last July. He was in the first army of Yanks of 8,000 men who checked the onward march of 300,000 Huns, and checked their advance toward Paris. The Bear River people are proud of their soldier boys."

## Chapter 10
## MA AND PA'S HELPERS
### By Ellen

Summer days were long because there was seldom any dawdling in bed. Johnny and I had to go and get the cows while the dew was still heavy on the grass. Some days the cows would hide in the thickest clump of brush and lie so still that there wasn't a tinkle of the cowbell to be heard. Sometimes we roamed all over the pasture, calling and searching. When we would finally give up and return home without them, there they would be, waiting at the barn door. Once in a great while, Ma would see them in the barnyard, or hear the sound of the bell, and then she wouldn't have to wake us quite so early.

Breakfast was seldom even thought of until after Ma, Laura and Johnny had milked the cows. I was usually in the house getting some of the younger ones dressed while the others were in the barn. Then, Ma stirred up a batch of pancakes or started making French toast or cereal.

On three mornings a week, Ma had to have the outgoing mail ready for Uncle Krist when he came by. Otherwise she did not need to be in the store in the morning hours. Customers seldom came in the morning because they were occupied with chores too. In the afternoon, her time could be taken up for hours. Sometimes a lonely bachelor would stay and talk long after he bought his few groceries, or some woman, yearning to chat with another woman, would walk three or four miles to buy a pound of 4X or Arbuckle coffee. If the lady had time, Ma would ask her into the kitchen for a cup of coffee and cookies before her long walk home.

The Russian and Polish women who lived west of us could not speak English well and sometimes resorted to words from their own language. Ma's speech had a strong Swedish accent, and she did not have the most extensive English vocabulary either but they managed to understand each other. Since Ma was always being called away by the sound of the little bell that announced the arrival of a customer, I had to take charge of things in the living quarters. Of course, I had to change diapers over and over again. I also recall sweeping the wide boards of the floor more than once or twice a day. When the kids had to be in the house, they cut paper dolls out of the catalog or just snipped little bits of paper that stuck to the rough floor. There was other cleaning to do and dishes to wash. Sometimes I was so busy that I would forget to put more wood in the stoves in cold weather. Then when Ma would return from a long chat with a customer, she would scold me for letting the fires get so low.

Laura and Johnny were Pa's helpers. They were supposed to be sawing lumber or stacking wood or putting up a new shed. There were times when they didn't work very steadily. At those times when I would see them making snowmen or just chasing each other around the yard, I resented having to make afternoon coffee and to set the table for them.

One day, Johnny made the mistake of complaining about how hard he had to work piling wood, while I stayed in the house and played with the kids. I think Ma knew who had the hardest job because she immediately suggested that Johnny and I exchange jobs for the afternoon. He really thought he was getting the better deal. "Oh, this will be easy," he said, as he began to gather up the dishes to wash them.

As I piled wood and enjoyed the peaceful quiet and the fresh air, I was able to relax my mind and dream to my heart's content. When we went into the cabin for afternoon coffee, we found a tearful Johnny. The table wasn't set, and the coffee and lunch were not ready. "I couldn't take care of the kids and get lunch ready too," he said between sniffles. "They mess up the house, and they mess up themselves. I'm always sweeping the floor or cleaning up one of the kids. And Ma has been in the store all afternoon!"

As he was talking, Ma came through the door from the store. "Johnny, are you already tired of your job?"

Since the trade was for all afternoon, I could have continued to pile wood, but the way the kids clustered around me, I knew they preferred their regular companion. Johnny was more than ready to go out and stack wood. That evening when everyone had come back in, he couldn't resist making a snide remark, "I had to straighten out the wood that Ellen piled."

Pa was quick to come to my defense, "Now Johnny, Ellen's work was just as good as any that you had done."

I heard often about the judgment of God on sinners, and I was told what a stubborn impossible child I was – and not at all like my perfect big sister. I know I tried to get out of my constant baby sitting job. I hid behind the shed and continued to play in the sand pile while Ma was calling, "Ellen, the baby is awake." I was always lugging a baby around. There was no crib or playpen, so when the current baby outgrew the buggy there was no place to put her except on the big bed after I had rocked her to sleep. It became a matter of moving slowly and carefully to put her down on the bed. Yet sometimes it didn't work. I remember pinching Helga when she woke up as soon as I had put her down on the bed. She screamed so loud that Ma came running in from the store. "What in the world is the matter with the baby?" Of course, I didn't know! So, I was a liar as well as a sneak.

Johnny knew he had to obey Pa, so he took his anger and frustrations out on me. He had a terrible temper, and when he got mad, I would run away screaming. Despite a fear of his reactions, I still liked to play tricks on him. One day in summer Pa gave Johnny orders to chop a huge pile of wood to have on hand for supplying a steam rig that would come in the fall to

PHOTO: Back: Ellen, Karl, Helga crying.
Front: Johnny and Laura.

thresh some shocks of grain. Of course, though Pa was proud of his field of grain, in reality it would be a small threshing job and wouldn't take that much to steam up for it. Maybe Pa thought that was one way of getting Johnny to chop more wood for winter use. My brother set to work on the big job. However, as soon as Pa was out of sight, Johnny would sit down and dream away the time.

One afternoon, after I had put the baby to sleep, I slipped quietly out of the house and saw Johnny sitting on his chopping block. He didn't see me, so I stepped behind the shed and called out in a gruff voice, *"Johnny, er dette hvordan du hakker tre?"* (Johnny, is this how you chop wood?) I was surprised that I had succeeded in imitating Pa's voice so well, for Johnny immediately jumped up, grabbed the ax and began to chop away for dear life. It struck me so funny that I burst out laughing.

Then the tables were turned on me. Johnny came running after me with ax in hand. I never screamed so loud nor ran so fast as I did then. At one point I was looking back to see if he was gaining on me and I ran right into the log wall of an unfinished building. That didn't stop me. I grabbed hand and toe holds between logs and shinnied right up to the top of the wall. Then I heard Johnny laughing. I looked down and saw that he had dropped his ax and was rolling on the ground because he was laughing so hard.

\*   \*   \*   \*

Winters were very cold in northern Minnesota, and I do not recall that I played outside at all in winter, until I started school. We did not have snowsuits or warm boots. Ma and Auntie made some very snug, warm and light moccasin-like footwear from any heavy warm pieces of material they happened to have on hand. They had a pattern, and the moccasin-boots were well-shaped. We wore them in the house, but of course they were not moisture-resistant, so they could not be worn outdoors.

Toward spring, when the snow was thawing, and the sun shone warmly through the windows, Karl and I would beg to go outside. Once in a while Ma would permit us to go out, but with the stipulation that we would stay on the wooden sidewalk Pa had built along one side of the house. We would run back and forth on the sidewalk for a while, but inevitably we would step off onto the soggy ground, or slushy snow. Whenever that happened, Ma would call us back into the house. One would think we would have had sense enough to stay on that sidewalk, but we never learned.

We knew exactly when summer began because that was the day Ma deemed it warm enough for us to take off our shoes and stockings and run barefoot in the grass. At first we walked very carefully on the road or other surfaces that were rough, but gradually our feet toughened and we could run anywhere. Only occasionally we would feel the very sharpest of stones. We remained barefoot all summer.

In summertime we often had picnics on the grass. In front of our log house was a lawn. We even had a manual push-type lawn mower that Pa had repaired after finding it on the dump in Hibbing. There was a tall flag pole in one corner of the lawn. On the Fourth of July, the flag was flying.

PHOTO: Nass School. Laura in center with a white dress and hair band, Johnny beside her. Many one-room schools sprang up in the region of all the homesteads.

I did not enter the first grade until the fall of 1918 after I was eight. I recall that a teacher had come to speak to our folks when I was six, and again when I was seven. Pa said, "No, it's too far – too hard for a kid her age to walk that far."

However, the lady who would be teaching at our school that fall after my eighth birthday, did not give up that easily. I hung around and listened because I wanted to go to school more than anything else in the world. I had visited school a couple of times and thought it was some kind of wonderland with all those maps and books and the magic blackboard on the wall.

My mother's next excuse was that I didn't have any shoes. When the teacher stated she could get shoes for me, Ma said, "Well, I can't get along without her to take care of the younger children."

I do not recall exactly what the teacher said, but she did remind my mother that there were laws about school attendance after the age of six – and I was already two years behind. Even so, my parents kept me at home for five or six more weeks. Pa kept Laura and Johnny home as many days a week as the law of attendance permitted. Laura wanted to keep up with her classmates but was always struggling to catch up. Johnny didn't care for school at all, so he was happy to stay home as much as he was permitted by Pa.

I had a very hard time learning to read, and our first grade Primer, as it was called, wasn't very exciting. I remember, "Jack can run" and "Jack can jump." The words "walk" and "talk" were also incorporated into the dry tale. I always tried to sound out every letter. The teacher would remind me that the letters that had a line drawn through them were "silent." I didn't know what "silent" meant. Up to the time I started school, I had only spoken our home mixture of Norwegian and Swedish. Spelling so often did not make sense. Why was not the "o" of "go" pronounced the same as the "o" of "do?"

Arithmetic was even harder to grasp than reading, but one day I thought I had discovered the secret of adding. The teacher had been giving me the basic addition facts in sequence: $1+1 = \_\_\_$, $2+1 = \_\_\_$, $3+1 = \_\_\_$, and on up to $9+1 = \_\_\_$. I found that I could get the right answer simply by starting with 2 and continuing on up to 10. She praised me for getting them all correct. The next day, however, when I used the same system, they were all wrong! Perhaps the teacher had guessed at my magic solution because they were not in sequence that time. I had a tough time, but I did catch up to the other two in the first grade.

Before the end of the year when I saw the bigger girls checking out books, I went to the shelves and selected the biggest book I could find. Of course, Laura and her pals laughed at me. Then the eighth-grade girl who was in charge of checking out our books, went to the well-stocked book shelves and found the smallest volume there. It was *Peter Rabbit*. There weren't very many other books for children in the first and second grades. Whenever we got a new reading book – and subsequent ones were of a much more colorful and interesting caliber than my primer – I would read all the stories and poems in it the first week or two. Soon I was reading fairy tales. There were the Japanese Fairy Tales, Grimms, and Hans Christian Anderson. I believe I was in the 3rd or 4th grade before I read *The Arabian Nights*. It's no wonder my nightmares continued to torture me. I also remember *Toby Tyler and the Circus, Sarah Graw, Heidi*, and *The Children's Bluebird*. I was always sad when school closed in May, because it meant the library books would not be available to me for three whole months!

Shoes were expensive items - a good reason for going barefoot in the summer. In September we would figure out what shoes we would fit into for the walks to school. We usually had to wear hand-me-downs, so I inherited Johnny's shoes. I thought Johnny would never outgrow the copper-toed shoes that I coveted every time I saw him wearing them. Finally they were too tight for him, so they were handed down to me. About that same time, my cousin Bertha got her brother's copper-toed shoes. It was a triumphant day for us when we first walked together to school wearing those copper-toed shoes.

When I was about age nine, I had such a persistent hacking cough that Ma and Pa feared I might have tuberculosis. A school nurse from the county seat was supposed to come sometime to check the school children, so every day when we came home from school, Ma or Pa would ask if the school nurse had been there. When the nurse finally came, it was a frightening experience for each of us who had never seen a nurse and had never been in a doctor's office or hospital. We stared with bulging eyes as she set up her equipment on the teacher's desk.

I don't know why I was called up there first, but I am certain that I was trembling clear down to my toes as I went and stood before her. She was not the kind that put a child at ease either. When she saw my hanky wadded up in my damp little fist, she snapped at me, "Don't you have some other place to keep your hanky? Drop it!" I heard the kids draw in their breath. She had an eye chart, so she first checked my vision. I could read everything easily, but some kids were found to need glasses. She put a dry-as-dust tongue depressor so far back on my tongue that I began to gag. Then she proceeded to poke around in my hair with a couple of little sticks. I could hear the gasps, giggles, and whispers all around the room. The nurse heard what they were saying because she said, "Yes, I am looking for vermin. If some of you get a notice to take home with you, it doesn't mean anything except that you happened to have some now. It is no shame to get them if you do something to get rid of them." Well, no one got a notice except for one family, but we knew that their mother wouldn't do anything about it anyway. Ma searched our heads constantly. If she happened to find any lice, she would rub in some strong-smelling powder.

Pa and Ma were glad to hear that the school nurse had finally been there. As we began to relate the happenings of the day, suddenly it all seemed very funny to us. We could hardly tell about it for laughing. The folks were disappointed. Now they would never know what caused my cough. [As I look back, I think it was a little tickle in my throat, or a real cough at first that probably became a habit, fed by a lot of attention and adult concern. I don't recall coughing at night, and it gradually disappeared entirely.]

Nightmares were another thing! They continued to disturb my sleep. It usually happened as soon as I dropped off. Ma would try to wake me and as I was coming out of it, I would see her bending over me, but she looked like some horrible creature with a distorted face.

Ma tried in many ways to cure me of my nightmares, but none of them worked. She first thought if I played hard enough after supper, I would be so tired that I would sleep too soundly for dreams. That didn't work, so she tried giving me a light supper and sending me to bed early. One such time was on a July 4th. I was already sleeping when Uncle Andrew's family and the Carlson family from the town of Virginia dropped by in the evening to share fireworks with us. Our cousin, Bertha, and friend Florence Carlson were with Ma when she came in to wake me. I put on my usual performance of screaming and fighting her off. It embarrassed Ma, and scared the girls. They were afraid to get near me, even after I was fully awake. I acted like a drug addict - which I probably was! My drug was caffeine. Ma did not think of depriving me of coffee until after she read an article in *The Farm* magazine about not letting children drink coffee.

My terrible dread of dying was also a part of my terror. I hated to waste any time sleeping because I had heard Ma say that we spent half of our lives sleeping – or a large fraction of it. Since life was so precious, and since I was so certain that I knew what waited for me after death, I intended to stay awake and enjoy every moment of my life. Besides, I knew I was not in control while sleeping, and I didn't know what might happen to me.

Pa's loud and penetrating voice reading lurid details of ax murders and other crimes didn't help to settle my nerves either. He did not read to us from the *Duluth Herald*, but when the same news came in the Norwegian weekly, *Decorah Poston*, he accepted it as authentic and newsworthy. I thought his favorite weekly was published in Norway. It wasn't until years later that I learned it was published in Decorah, Iowa.

## Chapter 11
## MORE CONVENIENCES YET BUSIER LIVES
### By Ellen

Pa loved having a car. It made trips to town much easier. The novelty made the news. The local Cook paper wrote, "Postmaster John Gilbertson was in from Nass Saturday afternoon on business. Mr. Gilbertson remarks that with a "Lizzie" and the good roads in his section he has little trouble in making the trip to town and home again after supper, which is quite an improvement on the old days." [A Model T was nicknamed a "Tin Lizzie."]

Yes, having the convenience of a car helped, but it also made life more hectic. As soon as neighbors and timber workers for miles around knew that we had a car, Pa was practically forced into the transportation business, simply because his was the only car within a ten-mile area. He gladly helped the neighbors and I eagerly rode along whenever possible.

After Pa fell asleep at the wheel one night while driving home from Cook, he always wanted someone to ride with him to talk and help keep him awake.

One extremely cold winter night, my enthusiasm for the Ford was nearly frozen out of me. That evening, two lumberjacks from a logging camp several miles west of us had come walking down to our store and asked Pa if he would take them to Hibbing. At first he said, "No," but they probably made him an offer he couldn't refuse, because he finally agreed to make the 40-mile drive. I was perhaps eight or nine years old at the time. I suppose I opened my big mouth and begged again to be the one to go along. I thought Johnny was all too eager to offer me his sheepskin jacket and boots. Ma put as many pair of wool socks on me as the big boots would accommodate. I had sweaters under the jacket and was so bundled up I could barely walk out to the car.

Of course there was no heater in the car, and the side curtains fastened with snaps, so the wind flapped and fluttered the curtains and whistled around my head. I drew my scarves as close as possible around my ears and neck, but I don't believe we had gone very many miles before I knew that I was getting cold – very, very cold. I don't know how much time went by before we reached Hibbing and dropped off the two men at their hotel. On those roads, I am certain it was at least two hours to make the forty miles.

I begged Pa to stop for a bowl of soup at the little Ford Cafe (no connection with the automobile.) It was a narrow building between two larger business buildings on Howard Street, and I knew they had good soup because we had stopped there before – in more pleasant circumstances. Pa argued faintly because he was afraid the radiator would freeze up. There was no anti-freeze, nor any cooling system for radiators, so they would freeze up in the winter and boil over in summer. I think Pa wanted some of that hot soup too, as he gave in to the suggestion after all. I don't think anything ever tasted so good or ran down to my tummy with such a warm feeling as did that soup. The car did start again and we were on our way. I managed to help Pa keep awake on the way home, or maybe he kept me awake. He talked to me and made me answer so I wouldn't go to sleep. Of course, by the time we got home, I was nearly too stiff from cold to get out of the car and waddle into the house. I wasn't as eager to volunteer for winter rides after that.

*   *   *   *

Life became busier yet when Pa bought a Case tractor and a saw mill. He could use the tractor to move the saw rig from one location to another. Also it was used to power the saw when cutting lumber for customers wherever they had a pile of logs. Johnny and Laura went with him to help with all the hard work. They came home once a week.

Laura had to quit school, much against her wishes. She was unable to finish the eighth grade because of infrequent attendance. Pa also kept Johnny at home as much as he dared to assist him at the saw mill. Attendance laws were not very strictly enforced back then, at least not way out in the northeast edge of Itasca County. The work was usually within a fifteen mile radius of home. Laura helped with the saw rig, but also did the cooking. One day she had cooked a fruit soup with raisins, prunes and dried apricots. Since her bowlful was too hot, she temporarily set it out on a stump to cool, as she went about her work. After a few minutes she returned to eat it, only to see a horse walking away with her bowl stuck on his nose.

    I was Ma's assistant, but she knew how much I hated to miss school, so she let me attend regularly. I even hiked down the road one morning when it was forty below zero. The three-quarters of a mile to the school seemed a long way when breathing in that arctic air. When it gets that cold, the snow creaks and crunches underfoot as if you were walking on potato chips. Twigs snap off trees with loud, crackling sounds. The telephone wires make a constant humming noise, which seems very, very loud and eerie, especially when you're one little kid alone. I did get to the school, but since I was the only pupil who came, the teacher let me go home after we had waited for half an hour.

    I mentioned telephone wires. There was no telephone service out our way until early in the 1920s when Pa and some other men along the route from Cook formed the Pioneer Telephone Company. Without pay and with little or no help, Pa put up most of the telephone line on the twenty-five miles from Cook to Nass. He had the hard work of digging holes to put in some high poles, but for the most part, he just tacked the lines to trees. The line had to follow the winding road most of the way. Pa also maintained it as he became the official line repairman. Since we were at the very end of the line, if our telephone was dead, Pa would have to trace it down. He would begin looking for the trouble spot as he drove eastward toward Celina. If their phone was also out, he knew we had to proceed farther. Usually he had Johnny, me, or both of us along to help look for broken wires or insulators. Johnny was better at spotting the trouble than I, because he knew what to look for. It was easy to spot if we would find that a tree had fallen across the line.

The business meetings of the Pioneer Telephone Company were usually held at night. One very cold night I accompanied Pa. The meeting was held in a beautiful home. The family there had nine girls, each named for flowers: Rose, Violet, Iris, Lilly, etc. On our way back home, the radiator froze up and we had to stop at a house along the road. Pa knocked on the door. A man who just got out of bed answered. The man did get us some hot water to thaw out the radiator, but he was very grumpy the whole time, annoyed by the inconvenience of the late intrusion.

As we drove on homeward, Pa said, "I noticed that family had a telephone, so they are enjoying the benefits of the line." Then he continued to lecture about the virtues of hospitality as practiced by the early pioneers. I was cold and sleepy, and as Pa talked, I was thinking about the beautiful home where the meeting had been held, and of all those nine girls in the home. Some were older than I and others younger. They had not seemed very friendly – but then, I was so shy and tongue-tied with strangers, it would have been impossible for anyone to carry on a conversation with me. So who was I to judge them?

Everyone in the community was relieved to know that in an emergency, he could come to our place to phone for a doctor. I remember when one neighbor, Mr. Danyluk, fell on the saw as he was sawing lumber. His son came and called the doctor. The doctor came from Cook, but there wasn't much he could do. He stopped on his way back to town. He was distressed and shook his head as he said, "The man was sawed nearly in half!"

\* \* \* \*

In time, more and more people bought cars of their own, so Pa wasn't transporting so many folk, but he could repair anything, so whenever neighbors had trouble with their cars, they came to him for help. In that way, too, our lives were busier. Since Laura was one of Pa's helpers, she learned quite a bit about the mechanics herself. One day a man came in with some kind of transmission problem. He had the gear that needed to be put in. When he learned that Pa was not home, Laura offered to put the gear in for him. The man did not want to trust his car to a girl, so he proceeded to do the work himself. Laura could see that he was putting it in wrong. She kindly tried to warn him, "If you put it in that way, you'll only be able to go in reverse."

The man had no intention of following her advice, so he made a mocking, "Humpf," and continued to put it in his way. Laura stood to one side and said no more. The man finished his job then backed out of the driveway. Without looking in Laura's direction he continued to back down the county road until he was out of sight. Sometimes a person's pride gets in the way.

A fairly good gravel road had finally been completed along the eastern edge of the homestead, making truck and car travel possible. With plans to relocate the house and store up by the road, Pa had already been building on the little hill by the big Norway pines.

Early in the summer of 1920, Pa's two bachelor brothers and his mother returned from Florida where they had lived for nearly five years. His father died down there because he had a problem with gallstones, but refused to have surgery.

Uncle Johan, who while in Florida had taken the more American sounding name of "Joe," liked horses and other domestic animals. He bought a team of horses soon after they returned. We liked Uncle Joe. He was a calm, kind-hearted, quiet and unassuming man.

Uncle Helge, or "Harry" bought a light truck. The two had worked in the oil fields in Oklahoma on their way back from Florida, so they had some money and wanted to settle down in the cooler climate. Pa wanted to sell them half of the land. Uncle Joe took over the farming operations on the homestead, while Pa continued to hammer and saw on the combination home, store and post office near the road. Meanwhile, the store and post office operated as usual in the log building down in the meadow.

Grandma Kari, or "*Farmor*" (meaning father's mother), helped with the cooking and washing the dishes, the milk pails, and the cream separator, but she always expected me to be on hand to wipe everything she washed. I was ten years old by that time. My babysitting job had also increased by the addition of a new baby brother, Ingvald Reinhold, born June 22, 1920.

With eight of us kids, our parents, Grandma and two uncles, thirteen in all, the house was over-crowded. It helped that the uncles set up their beds in one of the storage sheds. They hung their clothes in there and stored the belongings they had brought from Florida. Also in the summer, seven of us kids – all except the baby – slept out in what we called the summer bedroom, which was the woodshed that my father, Hans Skoglie, had built. After we all got into bed, we told stories until we were too sleepy to talk. One of us would begin the story, carry it on to a certain point, then call on someone else to take it from there. Johnny, age 12, was the best tale spinner, but just as he had us sitting up in bed, he would turn it over to me or Laura who was 14. Karl, 7, and Inger, 5, had to have their turn. The two younger ones Helga, 3, and Agnes, 2, would simply butt in, trying to add to the tale, even if it was unrelated. More often than not, they fell asleep before the others.

One afternoon, I walked up the hill with Ma to look at the new building. It was nearly finished. Pa, Laura and Johnny were putting some strong-smelling black paper on the outside. Ma didn't seem very happy. On the way home, she said, "It will never seem like home to me. It will be such a cold place with those single lumber walls covered by tarpaper."

After we moved from the log home to the house on the hill, it seemed as if life sped up even more. Perhaps it was because I was going on eleven, but it seemed as if the Fourth of July and Christmas had drawn closer together, and that Easter followed close on the heels of Valentine's Day. I also had to agree with Ma. Although we had more room in the big house, it was not as warm and cozy as the log home had been.

## Chapter 12
## "TIN LIZZIE" TRAVEL
### by Ellen

When Ingvald was only two weeks old, we took a long trip, or at least it was considered long in a "Tin Lizzie." We drove to Saginaw, near Duluth, to visit Emma, an old school chum of Ma's, whom she had not seen since she left Sweden. Emma had immigrated and moved to Saginaw after the Skoglies and Perssons had left for there.

We had hoped and planned for this trip ever since Pa got the Ford four years earlier.

During the winter before Ingvald's birth, Ma sewed several dresses for each of us five girls.

PHOTO: John Gilbertson's Model T. Sanna is at the left.

We could wear some new clothes on this trip. Laura had to stay home to take charge of the store and post office while the folks were gone. She would not be alone, since Grandma Kari and the uncles were there.

A hundred miles was a long distance in those days, especially if there were a few blowouts along the way. The first blowout came even before we got as far as Hibbing. While Pa patched the tire, Ma opened one of the lunch boxes, because we kids were already hungry. I suppose we had been too sleepy or too excited to eat breakfast. There must have been some mechanical trouble too, because I recall waiting while the car was being worked on in a large garage in Hibbing. Ma and we seven kids were permitted to sit in the showroom. All the shiny new cars fascinated us but not nearly as much as the shiny linoleum floor. When Ma wasn't looking, we tried it out and discovered that it was just as slippery as it looked! The old tires were still on the Ford as we drove out of there, for we had a few more blowouts before we got as far as Saginaw. We learned to expect it.

Ma had been so sure that once she got to the small town she would know exactly how to get to Emma's place, but a lot of changes had taken place since she had lived there in 1904 - sixteen years earlier. It seemed that we had been driving down one road and up another for hours. We six who were crowded in the back seat were getting restless since we were tired and hungry. We rode around Grand Lake and back to Saginaw, and she still could not find the road to Emma's place. Since by that time it was getting dark, Pa decided to park by the roadside, eat more of the sandwiches and cookies Ma had packed, and sleep in the car.

The old Model T Ford had no luggage compartment, but there was a storage place under the cushion of the back seat. Some luggage was between the front and back seat because Ma recalled that Karl slept hanging over a suitcase. Johnny and I in the back seat, made room for the three younger girls: Inger on the seat between us, and Helga and Agnes on our laps. I must have slept, too, because after listening to the croaking of frogs in the swamp beside the road, I suddenly realized it was daylight. The night had disappeared.

We drove a little ways and Pa stopped to question a farmer who was on his way to the barn to do his morning milking. It was only a short distance from there that we drove up a private road to a nice frame house on top of a little hill. We kids waited in the back seat, and Pa held the baby in the front seat, while Ma walked up to the kitchen door and knocked. A plump woman with a pile of brown hair on top of her head, opened the screen door. She looked puzzled, but as Ma talked, she clasped her hands, laughing and crying in true Swedish fashion. After they both shed a few tears, they came out to the car and Ma proudly introduced her family.

When we were all ushered into the house, Emma resumed her pancake making. She conversed with Ma as she worked. Suddenly I was very homesick. I wished heartily that I had stayed home with Laura and *Bestamor* (Grandma.) With no babies to take care of, I could have played more with my cousin, Bertha. Since there seemed to be no kids in this place, it would be a very dreary and long visit.

Then to my surprise, after Emma finished making her first batch of pancakes, she stepped briskly across the kitchen to the stairway that led up from the small living room. She yelled up the stairway. Soon girls began to appear. There was one who was older than I, one who was my age, ten, and two younger ones. It didn't take me long to discover that the one who was my age, considered herself far too superior to associate with me, but the 8-year-old girl, Huldah, had sparkling eyes and was a tomboy like me. We had a glorious time exploring the farm.

Like kids of all generations, we thought our parents were the strictest and most unreasonable of all, but I noticed a few things during that visit that caused me to change my mind. Huldah and I had been out roaming around while the others ate breakfast, so when we came back to the house, we had the table to ourselves. Huldah handed the syrup pitcher to me, before she used of it herself. I poured syrup on my pancake until it made a big puddle in the middle and oozed out over the edges, just as I always did at home. As I passed the pitcher to Huldah, I saw that she was staring at my plate in fascinated amazement. She glanced fearfully in the direction of the kitchen. She then dribbled thin little streaks here and there on her pancake. I realized they were not permitted to soak their pancakes with syrup the way we did in our home.

Huldah and I must have taken off as soon as we had eaten because she took me to a field of potatoes that seemed to reach for miles. We jumped across the rows and she warned me not to touch the plants. Then she said, "I'm so glad you came this morning because we were supposed to be pulling weeds out here today." I looked across the row upon row of potatoes, and I couldn't see any weeds.

Then I remembered what day it was. "But, it's Sunday," I said. We were not allowed to do any work on the Lord's Day, that is, aside from necessary jobs like milking cows, or feeding livestock. It is a day for worship and rest. Huldah only stared at me and shrugged, as if to say, "What difference does that make?"

The trip back home was uneventful except for more blowouts. It took many hours to get home, but we were glad we didn't have to spend another night sleeping in "Lizzie."

\* \* \* \*

The summer of 1920 was also the big blueberry summer. After Pa bought the car, he and Ma had taken blueberry picking jaunts every summer. Just beyond the Green Swamp on the way to Hibbing, they had found an old railroad grade on which the Ford could go far into the sandy, piney woods. There the blueberries grew more plentifully than in any spot they had ever found. The berries had never been as large or as plentiful as they were that summer.

Ma was a swift picker, and Johnny was a close runner-up, so he had been a berry-picker since the first summer they went there. I had been permitted one trial berry-picking day other summers, but I just dawdled along, ate most of what I picked and waited for lunchtime. That year, however, the berries hung like clumps of grapes. I so enjoyed picking! I could reap a handful every time, and my little pail filled fast. I picked twenty quarts that day and so did Pa, but Ma and Johnny picked forty quarts each. I know it must seem like the biggest berry-pickin' tale of the century, but it is the true-blueberry truth. We canned 400 quarts of sauce, besides jellies and jams. Other years we canned between 200 – 300 quarts at best.

Ma said she also wanted the little kids to see how the berries grew, so the last berry picking day of the season was enjoyed by the whole family, except Laura who stayed to tend the store. I didn't have much time to pick berries that day because I had to watch the little kids. The baby lay on a blanket, and I tried to keep the flies and bugs from walking all over his face. The other four picked berries for a while, but then they started playing and exploring. They were fascinated with some mysterious caves in the side of a sand hill, but Ma had warned me to keep the children away from them. "A bear might be in there," she cautioned. I was very busy, but thankfully there were no mishaps.

## Chapter 13
## OUR NEW HOME AND STORE
by Helga

We moved into the larger home on the pine-covered hill the fall of 1921. I, Helga, was only four years old when we moved. I recall crossing the field going eastward from our log home to get to the new one. My only recollection of that log cabin home is of rolling down a grassy hill with some of our cousins on a warm summer day. I can still picture my mother and Aunt Sarah standing together in the open doorway and laughing as they watched us at play.

In time, Dad took down the old log home and reassembled it on another location on the homestead for Grandma Kari and her two unmarried sons, Uncle Joe and Uncle Harry, to live in. We were glad to have our grandmother living nearby. We could see her place whenever we were playing outdoors.

By this time the church building had been constructed at Celina three miles east of our homestead. Reverend Fadum who had officiated at our grandparents' funeral, was the Lutheran priest. He had a church in Cook, but also served a circuit of three churches in the area where immigrants had settled: Celina, Bear River, and Silverdale. He faithfully ministered in this pioneer region for forty years – from 1906-1946.

PHOTO: Reverend Fadum

When growing up in Norway, my father had sung bass in a church choir where his family and grandparents had attended, but now he did not attend regularly. He wanted the family to attend the Celina Lutheran Church whenever possible. Not that he had a personal active faith at the time, but rather insisting they go there simply because "Norwegians are Lutheran." When we would attend church together I always remember Grandma Kari's beautiful high soprano voice

PHOTO: Erik Holte and Kari, my father's mother.

singing on the hymns. In 1924, four years after Grandma's return from Florida, she married Erik Holte, who was a brother to her first husband Gulbrand Johnson. They had different surnames because Erik chose to be called Holte, after their farm name in Norway. We called him Grandpa, but we feared him. He drank and was a mean man. Once when we children were all sick in bed with the mumps, Grandpa Holte came to visit. I heard him approaching, so I quickly hid under the bed. He mockingly laughed at the plight of the sick ones. My heart was pounding as I tried to keep from sneezing because of the dust under the bed, but I stayed hidden until he left.

    The new store and attached home was constructed of two by fours and lumber with "tarpaper," a black roofing material on the outside. Most people put siding on their homes for warmth as well as for appearance. Ours was never finished on the outside all the years we lived there so it was literally and truly a huge tarpaper shack. The inside had blue building paper covered with wall paper. There was no such thing as insulation between the walls at that time and we had no storm windows either. The house was never comfortably warm in winter, even with a pot-bellied stove in each room. (20-45 F degrees below zero is common in a Minnesota winter. On rare occasions, it gets down to 50 or even 60 below!) No wonder Mom used to long for the cozy warmth of her former log cabin home!

    We had a big living room in which Dad painstakingly laid hardwood flooring. Its boards fit together perfectly. That floor was easy to keep clean, but it also made a good skating rink in the wintertime. We had no entry hall. As we had no storm door either, we easily tracked snow in by the door and it froze there. We did have many a good laugh at some unsuspecting grown-up who would come in and slide into the room.

We had no comfortable living room furniture, but what we had was genuine "early American!" The table, made of sturdy boards, was big enough to seat twelve people around it. We had unique chairs – each one different. They had been factory made - probably in the dark ages. Some had broken rungs, others had broken backs. Except for a couple of factory-made library tables and the pot-bellied heating stove, that was the total of our living room furniture. Mom loved green, growing things and had many pots of geraniums on a table by the window.

The kitchen was small. It contained the cast iron cook stove and the wood box, a small stand for the water pails and a wash bowl, a table for kneading bread dough or for other food preparations, a cream separator, and two homemade cupboards. One of the cupboards had doors and was used for food storage; the other, open except for a bright cretonne curtain across it, was used for dishes. There weren't any plastics in those days, so there were odds and ends of cracked plates and cups without handles. Another shelf was reserved for Mom's best dishes that were used only when we had company. Other shelves stored pots and pans, linens, stationery, etc. Dish towels were made from bleached flour sacks which Mom embroidered. An old-time country kitchen would not be complete without a slop pail

PHOTO: Store and Post Office at Nass

in which to empty the washbasin or dishpan.

We did not have indoor plumbing, but we did have hot water! Our range had a reservoir that held ten or twelve quarts for washing hands or dishes. Besides, there was always a full teakettle on the stove. Woe to the one who forgot (sometimes conveniently) to refill the reservoir after the dishes were done! The trouble was, the water pails always seemed to be empty. We had to fill them at the hand pump outside. During most of the winter that meant two of us had to put on boots, coats, hats, and mittens to get the water. One had to prime the pump - pour warm water so it would run inside the pipe and thaw it out - and the other had to keep pumping until the water came up. After replenishing the reservoir and teakettle, the pails had to be refilled. All this went well - except for the times the carrier slipped on the ice by the door and spilled it all.

People may talk of the "good old days," but I did not think they were so wonderful, especially when thinking of trekking to an outhouse in 30 or 40 below zero weather. Brrr! They may have been good times in ways of families doing things together, but as for comforts - or the lack of them - I do not wish to have those days back.

There were two large bedrooms. We had to go through one to get to the other. In each room were several beds with iron bedsteads. It wasn't solid iron, but open-work that resembled filigree, in ornate designs – scrolls etc. They were painted white. The springs and mattresses were so worn that they looked more like hammocks than beds. However, we did have enough good bedding to keep us warm. Mom made wonderful comforters out of wool batting with flannel on the back and colorful cotton print on top. She pieced together sheets out of bleached flour sacks. Pillow cases were of the same material, but she embroidered and crocheted on them so they were pretty.

There were no built-in closets, but each room had a big homemade wardrobe. Actually, one was made out of the old fold-down bed that had been used in the original cabin. There was a dresser in one bedroom but only a small table in the other, on which to set the kerosene lamp at bedtime.

In the middle room there was a trap door leading to the root cellar. There all of our garden produce was stored in bushel baskets that were perched on an earthen ledge to keep them cool. There were some shelves, too, where our canned goods like the 300 quarts of blueberries, pickled vegetables and jams and jellies were stored for winter use. When it would rain a lot, water would seep into the cellar. One of our chores after the rains was to take turns pulling the handle of the pump that Dad had rigged up to draw the water out of the cellar.

One day Laura was helping Mom do some canning. She went with some jars in hand to carry down into the cellar. The staircase was so steep that it was little better than a ladder. Despite being careful, Laura fell down the stairs. Mom's initial reaction was, "Oh no! Did you break any jars?" Thankfully Laura wasn't hurt, and neither were any jars broken, but we all teased Mom for her reaction, as if she didn't care whether or not Laura got hurt. Later I had to consider, if I were in her shoes, trying to keep a big family fed, I may have thought of the food first too.

We also had an attic. A steep staircase led up to it. The narrow room with its low ceiling, sloped at the sides by the angle of the roof, had a window on the east end over the store. The old blue trunk from Sweden was stored up there. Mom also had a big loom there on which she wove nice rugs out of rags. It was too hot in summer for Mom to spend time weaving rugs in the attic, and it was too cold there in the dead of winter, so she had to do it when the weather was between the extremes. We had many rag rugs throughout the house, except by the door in winter, where it just froze to the floor. Whenever one of us wore a brightly colored new dress, Mom would remark, "What nice colored stripes that will make in a rug someday!" We used to laugh at Mom - or should I say "with Mom" since she laughed just as heartily as we did, because it was as if she couldn't wait for the dress to wear out.

We had a door from our living room into the post office and store. That was a large area, probably 30 X 16 feet in size, with the post office at one end. There was a waiting room with benches for the customers, and a stove to keep it comfortable in winter. The waiting room had one outside wall, and was enclosed by counters on two sides. The fourth side had post office boxes nearly to the ceiling.

On the counter was a Dayton Scale and a roll of brown paper for wrapping up the purchases of the customers. There was also a big ball of twine on a spindle to tie up those purchases. There were no big brown bags as we would get in grocery stores later, but we had tiny brown bags in which to weigh out a nickel's worth of candy. We had big covered candy pails under the counter. We also had glass candy cases on top of the counter for 5 cent candy bars and gum. I remember Bit-O-Honey, Babe Ruth, Hershey bars, as well as Spearmint, Juicy Fruit, and also Bloodberry gum, which was red in color. Cracker Jacks at 5 cents, and Smith Brother's Cough Drops were included in the case.

Flour, sugar, and rice were sold by the pound out of 100 pound sacks. There were also some cookies sold by the pound out of wooden boxes. Prior to that, Ellen remembers selling crackers, rusks (like hard toast), and soap powder by the pound out of wooden barrels. There were boxes of powdered sugar, brown sugar, raisins, prunes, rye crisp, graham crackers, and soda crackers (years after the disappearance of the old cracker barrel.)

We liked to stock the shelves to help Mom when the big boxes came from Stone Ordean Wells. We had all the ordinary household necessities such as soda, baking powder, salt, pepper, pearl barley, vanilla, molasses, vinegar, Karo Syrup, jam, jelly, and peanut butter. Cinnamon and other spices were also available.

The Arm and Hammer Soda still has the same box design as it did in 1923! The syrup, jams, and jellies were sold in half-gallon pails, which were ideal for the large families of that day. Besides, when empty, these nice shiny pails served as lunch buckets to carry to school. Whenever we would open a new pail, the arguments began concerning which one of us would get the new pail as soon as it was empty.

Our farmer customers didn't need to buy dairy products,

but we stocked canned milk on the shelf for the occasional bachelor who wanted to buy it.

We were proud to sell the first ready-made cereal, Kellogg's Corn Flakes, but we also stocked the old favorites: Oatmeal, Farina, and Cream of Wheat. There was cocoa, tea, and coffee. There were no tea bags. Loose tea leaves were in one-pound packages. Coffee was sold as whole beans. Every home was equipped with a coffee grinder and it was always ground fresh just before brewing a pot of coffee. I can still see in my mind's eye, an advertising slogan on the wall in the store: "Good Morning! Have you had a cup of EMPRESS COFFEE this morning?"

Without refrigeration, we were unable to sell fresh meat, but we did sell salt pork by the pound from a big slab. In the summer, we had the long summer sausages as well. We sold canned meats: corned beef, sardines at 5 cents a tin, anchovies, salmon, and big tins of fish balls, and of beef. It was after World War I that we were able to get the large tins of surplus beef that became very popular with the customers. We also used a lot of them ourselves.

On shelves at the farthest end of the store were men's work gloves and men's socks, as well as kerosene lamps and lanterns, flashlights, candles, batteries, wicks, lamp chimneys, and various other hardware items too numerous to mention. There were some home remedies such as: castor oil, cough syrup, Sloan's liniment, Vick's VapoRub and Vaseline.

After a few years at the new place, mail came by truck and we were able to order Zinsmaster Bread, cinnamon rolls, and doughnuts from a bakery in Duluth. We kids thought it a great treat when the bread began to mold. Then we could cut out the mold and toast the bread. "Boughten bread," as we referred to it, was something special!

Bachelors were very happy with the convenience of bakery bread. One Finnish bachelor would come in and ask for *"mooste lepe"* (brown bread.) Some of the Russians would ask for *"хлеб"* (bread). Through the years, there were some who never learned English. They would point to what they wanted to buy. Mom would tell them what it was called in English.

Sometimes she learned the word in their language: Slavanian, Russian, Polish, Ukrainian, German, or Finnish, and would say it in their language. They were pleased and were comfortable with her. When they didn't understand what they owed, they just laid their coins on the counter trusting Mom to take the correct amount and not cheat. There must have been close to 150 people who received service at our store and post office.

Another room was added to the store that we "brilliantly" called the oil room since it contained barrels of oil sold by the quart. It also had a barrel of kerosene, kegs of nails, staples necessary for repairing fences, plus fan belts, tires, and other car parts needed for repairing Model T Fords. Outside this room stood a gas pump. I remember gas being as high as 25 cents a gallon.

When roads were improved and many were driving cars, Uncle Krist, too, had bought a car, so he was able to take the outgoing mail to Cook and return with the incoming mail all in the same day. Mondays, Wednesdays, and Fridays were the mail days, so now he had a day off between trips.

Mail days were exciting days. It was a time for all the folks in the community to get together with neighbors and socialize while waiting for the mailman to come. As the men sat and smoked their pipes and cigarettes, they had a noisy good time, talking and laughing. We children also enjoyed the excitement, but we were not to set foot in the store or post office at those busy times. We were permitted to stand in the open doorway from the living room, as long as we kept quiet.

The men used the occasion of mail days as an excuse to drive their shiny Model Ts. Fords came from both directions.

PHOTO: Left-right: Agnes, Inger, Ed Gilbertson's brother, John, Karl giving a dog a ride on a cart, Helga, and Ingvald. The water pump is to the right of the steps.

They started arriving long before mail time so they could fill up their gas tanks, or buy groceries, mail a package, buy a stamp or money order. As for the cost of postage in the 1920s, it was the day of a penny postcard. You could actually buy a stamped card for one cent. It took a two cent stamp to mail a letter. You could buy a stamped envelope for three cents, or two for five cents.

Some people also came hoping for a package since every family found it convenient to order merchandise from Sears Roebuck, Montgomery Ward, or M.W. Savage. When Uncle Krist arrived, lugging in the big canvas sacks, Mom had to unlock them. The key was on a long chain, the end link of which was stapled into a drawer so the key could never come up missing. She would dump the bags upside down on the floor and begin sorting it, and placing it into the proper boxes.

Decades later, Inger found a copy of a legal paper for the mail route in the 1920s. The dates on that contract were July 1, 1923 to June 30, 1927. Krist received $1,075 annual salary. (By the way, the price of a Model T in 1923 was $319) When that contract expired, Uncle Helge, or "Harry" as he came to be known, took over the mail hauling with his truck. The roads were fine unless it rained. There were several low places on the route where, after a couple of hard rains, the mud would ooze up and overpower the thin gravel. We learned to expect the mail truck to be late on rainy days.

PHOTO: Uncle Harry's home (Left to right) Mom (Sanna), Horace, Berdetta, Uncle Harry, Grandpa Erik, and Grandma Kari

Uncle Harry had been corresponding with Berdetta, a widow whom he had met while down south. When he proposed by mail, she and her two sons, arrived by bus and she and Harry got married. Mom saw that the sleeves of the boys' outgrown sweaters were too short, so she knitted extensions onto the sleeves. The smiles on the boys' faces showed their gratitude for her kindness. Berdetta had a hard time adjusting to the long cold winters in northern Minnesota.

*   *   *   *

One hot summer day, the sheriff's car stopped on the road not far from our home. We went to see what was happening. The sheriff saw us following and said, "You kids go back home!" Scriptures tell us, *"Obey them that have the rule over you..."* (Heb.13:17a). We should have obeyed, but out of curiosity, we followed at a distance. He and his deputy went into the woods where a man had purportedly hanged himself. The body was not hanging but was in a sitting position on the ground with a rope around his neck. The rope was tied to a small spruce bough. Even we knew there was no way such a spindly limb could have supported the weight of a man, even if it had been eight feet off the ground, which it wasn't. It was believed that the body was placed there after death. The features were those of a white man, but now he was black, decomposing with the passage of time in sweltering summer heat. The sheriff and his deputy placed the body into a canvas bag and returned to town with it. We never learned the identity of the man.

We turned and went back home before the sheriff knew we were watching, but we were sorry we hadn't obeyed when he had told us to go home. We could have spared ourselves the gruesome sight and the thoughts that would plague our minds.

We were reminded that evil is around, even in the peaceful North Woods. We ourselves had some close calls and gave thanks to God for sparing us from evil intents, or from injuries.

# Chapter 14
# CLOSE CALLS

**Danger at the Saw Mill - by Helga**
One cold fall morning when we younger kids were pretty small, we all walked to where Dad had set up the saw mill. When Inger saw the white frost on the blade of the circular saw, she tried to lick it. Her tongue immediately froze to the saw blade. Every kid in the north has done the same thing at one time or another, when seeing frost on anything metal. The danger was, Dad had just gone into the shed to start up the motor to run the saw. Inger could be badly injured or killed. Several of us ran immediately toward the shed to try to stop him. We were all yelling at once, causing quite a racket, "Dad, Dad, STOP!" "Don't turn it on!" Karl, who had reacted the quickest, reached Dad first and explained the problem.

Dad was very relieved we caught him in time. He instructed Karl, "Run to the house fast and bring back some warm water." This way he could free Inger without tearing flesh from her tongue. All of us were glad that Dad knew what to do. Inger was in agony until she could be freed. It was a lesson for us all never to be tempted to lick the frost on anything metal.

**The Stranger in the Night - by Helga**
Something unexplained and eerie happened to us one summer night. To this day, we still wonder about it. Our tarpaper building was very hot at night and we girls decided to sleep in our playhouse. It also was a tarpaper shack but it did get some shade from trees and since it was only 8x10 in size, it cooled off better than the house did. The playhouse was in the edge of the woods, and about 250 feet away from the road and the house.

Laura was still away, working at the saw mill so there were four of us girls. We had a double bed with a homemade trundle bed under it that we pulled out at bedtime. That way, we slept comfortably but had room to dress after pushing the trundle bed underneath in the morning. One evening, since Inger had gone to stay overnight with her cousin, Elva, and Agnes wanted to stay with Mom, it was only Ellen and I who went to bed in the playhouse. It was a moonless dark night.

When we were nearly asleep, we were vaguely aware of hearing heavy footsteps outside. Yet already being so far removed from consciousness, we felt no fear or apprehension and drifted off to sleep. Suddenly, we both snapped awake and simultaneously sat up. It had previously been pitch dark, but now our eyes were fixed on something white in the room. Ellen said, "Helga, did you hang a white dress on the chair?"

"No, I wasn't wearing white."

"It must be the curtains blowing in" she said, her voice a bit shaky.

My words came out in a hoarse whisper, "But the curtains are brown!"

The white thing became more elongated and moved toward us.

"Who are you?" Ellen asked. I felt proud of her for being so brave.

No answer.

She repeated, "Who are you? What do you want?"

Still no answer. The long white shape moved towards the door then just evaporated.

Ellen said in a matter-of-fact voice – as much to calm herself as to reassure me, "I think we'd better go back to the house!" It was frightening to go outside when we didn't know what danger lurked out there, but it was more frightening to stay. So, we found the courage to go. When we got to the house, Karl said he was working on a car with the aid of a flashlight just at dark and he said he saw someone in white hurrying between the trees in the direction of our sleeping quarters. He thought it was Aunt Sarah, or that Inger had come back.

The following morning, we found that our lamb which had been kept in a sturdy pen close to our sleeping cabin, was out of its pen. Another pen nearby was also empty. We had to hunt for the calf that belonged in that one.

We guessed what may have happened. A neighbor's

grown son, Art, was mentally deranged. His parents told us he had done many strange things. It is possible that Art was walking around our cabin and found the pens with the lamb and the calf. He was one who was disturbed whenever he would see an animal penned up. He was extra strong and may have lifted them out of their pens to free them. I wonder what might have happened if this crazed one had found us "penned up" in the small building? I believe we may have been visited by a guardian angel who was urging us to leave before we would be harmed!

Only a day or two later, Art stood inside the door of his home with an upraised ax, waiting for his parents to return from their barn chores so he could murder them. Luckily, they saw his shadow in time and did not enter the house. They called the sheriff and had him committed.

## Inhaling Gas Fumes - by Helga

One time a 'gas man' came and was filling the buried gas tank by the store. Two-year-old Ingvald put his mouth over a pipe sticking out of the ground. He got gas or fumes into his system and became very sick and was vomiting. Ellen lovingly carried him around all day. The next day he was okay.

## Bear Scare - by Helga

One night as the kerosene lamp shed its soft glow of light in our bedroom, my sisters and I were getting ready for bed. Suddenly there was a thump and a rattle of the window panes. We all immediately turned to look at the tall window. A huge bear was there, standing upright with its front paws outstretched to the uppermost corners of the window. His beady eyes were surveying our room through the thin panes of glass. We all screamed and ran from the room. Simultaneously, the bear made an eerie screeching sound as his long claws scratched on the glass.

Our dad quickly came to investigate, but by then the bear was gone. Uncle Krist had shot a bear in 1924. I wished that this bear could also be killed, so I wouldn't have to worry about it coming back again. With hearts still beating wildly, we hesitantly returned to our bedroom and crawled beneath the covers on our beds. Sleep eluded me. My 9-year-old mind kept replaying the frightful image of the bear. It would have taken so little for that bear to break right through the window. Mom comforted us, urging us to say our prayers, and trust in God to protect us.

Shortly after that, Dad had a nightmare that a big bear was in the room. Dad was determined to kick him out. He took a good swing at it and WHAM! His foot hit the wall - a painful awakening. At breakfast, when we kids heard about it, we laughed - but Dad didn't. His foot was sore for a long time.

## The Abduction - by Helga

There was a man, John Maronic, operating a saw mill in the vicinity, who would come to the post office for his mail. He was not a likeable man, at least from a child's point of view, but the men liked to joke with him, and he with them. One day, Inger, then about age nine, disappeared for hours. Mom had discovered that Inger was missing and was very worried! She had suspicions about Maronic. Perhaps it was a mother's intuition, but she didn't trust him around children. Entering the store she inquired if anyone had seen Inger. They all shook their heads. "How about Maronic," she asked. "He was here, wasn't he?"

"Yes, he was. He was showing off his new car. He's gone now."

Neighbors immediately helped search for the girl in the nearby woods, but she could not be found. Finally, as it was getting dark, Inger came home. She related what had happened. The man had offered her a ride. She had happily gotten in, thinking she could boast about her ride in the new car. Before they had gone very far, he showed her a knife with a long shiny blade and said, "You do what I say, or I'll kill you with this and cut you in pieces."

As soon as he slowed the car to stop, she leaped out and ran. She darted through the trees, and thick brush to stay out of sight of her pursuer. Finally when she could no longer run, she hid under a rotten log in a swamp. She lay there with her heart racing, listening for any sound of the man approaching. She didn't dare move for hours for fear he would find her. When, at last it was getting dark, Inger ventured out of her hiding place and stealthily made her way back home. The family was grateful she had not been physically harmed, but of course she was very emotionally shaken.

## Thieves - by Ellen

Every summer Ma enjoyed working out in the garden, just to be away from the kids, the housework, and the store. I dreaded having to step into the business quarters and deal with customers, but I didn't mind the post office work quite as much. There I could at least hide behind the tall cabinet. I learned how to insure packages, register letters, sell stamps, and make out money orders before I was thirteen. Of course, I had to use Ma's name and sign my initials under it.

One day, when I was fourteen, I heard the bell in the store. It was early morning when we seldom had customers. I knew Ma was out in the garden, so I stepped in there and saw a strange man at the money order window. He was sticking his head as far as he could through the little opening as he tried to look behind the counter. When he saw me, he said he wanted a money order. I gave the secret signal to one of the kids standing in the doorway, indicating to go get Ma. Being so early, the money order books - even the one with most of the blanks gone - were still locked in the safe. As I twirled the dials, I glanced back. The man was staring right at me, but I had my back to him, so he couldn't have seen the combination. I grabbed the half-used book, slammed the door shut and turned the dials to lock the heavy door.

I was wondering what was taking Ma so long, but hadn't considered she would stop in the kitchen to wash her hands. I felt ill-at-ease with the man. It was odd that he requested a money order for only 69 cents. I had just finished making out the money order when Ma stepped in from the family quarters. She was a trifle upset at me for calling her in from the garden, but when she saw the stranger at the post office window and another man sitting in a car with the motor running, she was all attention. I handed the money order to the man. He paid me, then turned to leave. While he made his way out, he was looking sharply in all directions, as if trying to memorize the layout of the place.

As the car drove away, we stared through the double windows over the old table that served as a desk in the post office. Ma shook her head, "Well, I certainly don't blame you for calling me in this time. There is something very suspicious about those two! And such a small money order!"

The next day we heard that the post office ten miles south of us had been robbed of all its money order books. It was the same two men who stopped there. While the postmaster/storekeeper had been outside pumping gas in their car, one of them asked, "Can I use the telephone?"

The postmaster said, "Sure, go in and help yourself." So he did! It wasn't until some patron came to buy a money order that they discovered the books were missing.

Soon after that, we had a visit from the postal inspector and a detective. Ma called me in to tell them about the two strange patrons. For once I wasn't shy as I described the man. I suppose I felt very important, and even more so when the detective turned to the inspector and said, "Hmm. Sounds like Boston Blackie, doesn't it?"

They laughed about the other postmaster telling the man to go in and help himself. They praised Ma for keeping the books in the safe, and me for noticing their strange behavior, and for locking the safe as soon as I had taken out the one book. As far as noticing their strange behavior, we all noticed anyone that was not of the immediate community, and would have been just as cautious and curious if it had been an honest farmer from a nearby community.

We never did hear any more about our early morning visitors. It takes a long time to track down and capture those who steal money orders because they do not use the stolen order blanks for years. Money orders are numbered. The numbers of stolen ones are listed and sent to every post office. There are thousands of stolen ones on file. After a few years the thieves try to cash some of them. No order can be written for more than one hundred dollars, yet back then that was three months' wages.

## Ruptured Appendix - by Ellen

I also had a close call with my health problems. From the time I was eight years old I had some attacks of indigestion that grew more and more frequent and increased in severity and agony through the years. I remember the first one I had. It happened on Easter Sunday. I had eaten three or four eggs, and after dinner we were playing in the hayloft. Pain grew steadily worse and worse. Finally I had to lie down in the hay. I suppose I was groaning and moaning because the other kids also dropped down on the hay and moaned and groaned as they rolled restlessly about. They said they were so full that their stomachs hurt too. When they got tired of teasing me, and tired of playing, they went back to the house, but I continued to lie there until I was able to move without feeling so much pain.

After a couple of years and several more attacks, Pa took me into the town of Virginia to see the same doctor who had operated on him for gallstones. The doctor pushed my belly down to the backbone, prodded and pried and finally ruled out appendicitis. Then he asked Pa if I ate a lot. Pa just shrugged his shoulders. Finally the doctor said, "Aw, there's nothing wrong with her. Take her home and don't let her eat so much."

Since Pa had so much faith in the doctor, he naturally took his diagnosis as gospel truth. After that, whenever I had one of my sick spells, he would tell me to quit acting. Ma knew I was not acting. She continued to insist that they get another opinion. Finally they took me to a doctor in Two Harbors on Lake Superior. He likewise found no indication of appendicitis. Pa insisted that the doctor give me the same medicine he had given Uncle Krist. The doctor only looked troubled and said, "It wouldn't do her any good."

Nevertheless, after we got home, Pa had me take that medicine before every meal. I still remember its bitter taste. I did my best to forget, but Pa always reminded me. The attacks then came more often than ever.

Finally, in March of 1925, when I was nearly fifteen, I had such a painful attack that Ma sent one of the kids to the sawmill to get Pa. "Tell him that he has to take Ellen to the hospital right away!" Since I could not sit up, they put quilts and pillows in the back of the pickup truck – one of Pa's most recent purchases. Laura sat back there with me.

We were only about two miles from home when the pain and pressure suddenly released as if something had burst. I told Laura, "Tell Pa he can turn around and go home because the pain has stopped."

I could hear his voice through the lifted curtain of the back window. I was surprised to hear him say, "No, then we had better hurry to the hospital." He knew my appendix had ruptured. He probably suspected the cause of my attacks all along, but tried to avoid thinking of the expense of another surgery.

The ordinary big white house with a canoe tipped upside down on the front porch, didn't look much like a hospital. The front room was a reception room with a desk at one end. A short, rather chubby man in a bathrobe peered at me over his glasses. Of course, it was getting rather late in the evening and we got him out of bed, or from his easy chair in another room. Pa reminded him, "I brought her in before, and the doctor definitely ruled out appendicitis, and now it probably has ruptured!"

The man told Pa and Laura to bring me into the examining room. There he pushed my stomach in until I was ready to scream. The doctor was speaking to Pa as he examined me, "You mean you can't pay anything now - nary a penny?" I saw him standing over me, and I heard the words, but was too groggy to fully grasp why money was such a big issue. I suppose he had to wait so long before Pa had paid his own surgery in full that he wasn't anxious to take on another long-term deal. Yet, after some grumbling and protesting, he finally agreed to operate in the morning. Upstairs was a plump nurse who put an ice bag on my side.

I came out of it in the morning and saw a strange room and a strange man sitting by my bed, reading a magazine. His head came up with a jerk, "Oh are you awake already?" he said. He stepped over to the door and called the nurse.

I was in that small hospital nearly three weeks. My cousin, Sally - the one born in 1905 shortly after Uncle Andrew and Aunt Sarah arrived in America - was there having her first baby. She was married quite young and lived in Cook where her eldest sister, Christina, also lived with her husband and family. While I was recuperating, the nurse brought in the baby, Betty Jane, to show her to me, but I never did see Sally. Helmer and his wife stopped in to see me after they had visited Sally in her room. It was pleasant knowing that one of my cousins was so near. At times I was homesick.

A neighbor girl who was working in town, came to see me on her evenings off from work. She wanted to bring me books from the library, but a nurse told her they would rather furnish me with magazines they had in the hospital. They brought me some. *Redbook* was one of them. The stories were very tame compared to what is being published now, but still they were probably not what my mother would have approved.

The nurses kidded me about the school subjects I should be studying. It is true, I would have been wiser to have had my civics, history, geography, and other textbooks brought to me, but I knew I could catch up. I truly think I would have, but shortly after getting home I developed an enormous sty on one eye. It was more than a sty because my eye swelled into a ball that I couldn't open in the mornings. Ma didn't let me do any reading while I was convalescing at home. Even after three weeks when I did try to go to school, I had to quit again. The teacher told Ma, "She will only strain her other eye if she continues to study by covering the bad eye." By the time I was better, and could study, there were only two or three weeks left until final exams. I studied hard and when I took the exams I felt certain I had made a passing mark. I was very disappointed when I only passed two of the six subjects. Some of the other classmates did no better. Another teacher in a school west of us told Ma how our teacher graded and that we could have had a better chance of passing if we could have sent our own papers to the County Board ourselves.

I had begun to gain weight before my surgery – actually, ever since Ma read an article in *The Farmer* that advised parents to let their kids drink whole milk, and give the skim milk to the calves and pigs. Also, it advised against letting kids drink coffee. Then after my surgery, I ate freely without the fear of those dreadful attacks. I enjoyed good health and good digestion, but I overdid – or overate - and gained weight.

I felt self-conscious about my awkward size but, nevertheless, I did attend school with all the younger children that fall. That year we had an older teacher with many years of experience. At first, she watched me closely, probably assuming I would not do my work since I had not passed some of my subjects the previous year. Since I was the only one in the eighth grade, I had to answer all the questions in class, which I did at length, especially in history because I liked that subject. Finally one day, when my teacher came up to the post office to get her mail, she told Ma, "I can't understand why Ellen hadn't passed. She is one of the best pupils I have ever had."

## Chapter 15
## CHRISTMAS TIME
### by Helga

We had wonderful times at Christmas. Although we did not have material wealth, and lacked what some would consider necessities, we had a wealth of love and fun in our family. We also had many of our extended family nearby – cousins, aunts, uncles, and grandparents to enjoy. I don't mean to say that we didn't have disagreements and even fights among us kids, because we certainly did! We're grateful we had parents who disciplined us when we needed it, yet I would assume we were likely on our good behavior at Christmas time.

We decorated early for the season, putting cedar boughs behind mirrors and pictures. It looked pretty, plus the cedar gave off such a fresh fragrance. We hung red and green crepe paper streamers with red bells on the ceiling too. The tree was put up early so we could enjoy it longer, and we all helped trim it. I liked the tinkling bells and the treetop angel best of all. Since we did not have electricity, our tree was lighted with candles, but they were only lit on the most special days – Christmas Eve, Christmas morning, and New Year's Eve.

Before I was school age, I remember the excitement of the Christmas programs. We rode in the Model T Ford three miles to the Celina Lutheran Church. We did not attend regularly, but we went several times a year, I guess whenever Dad was in the mood. When we entered the church, we stared at the huge tree, all lit up with candles. During the program, each of us children said a "piece" in Norwegian. There was a play with the manger scene and many carols were sung. When it was time to leave, they gave us each a bag of candy and nuts.

There was also a program at our one-room school, three quarters of a mile from our home. Since that program was always on a week night, Dad was not at home, so we walked to the school. I remember being bundled up warmly and walking when the stars were shining brightly. One time it was bitter cold. The two youngest, Agnes and Ingvald, were wrapped in blankets and placed in a sled, but there was not room for me. I was probably four or five years old then. I was peeking over a woolen scarf that covered most of my face, just as my brothers and sisters were doing. The snow creaked loudly underfoot, as it always does in bitter sub-zero cold. We must have sounded like a herd of cattle stampeding. It seemed to me that we had been walking for hours when we finally got to the school. It was good to get inside where it was nice and warm and to see many of our neighbors who had arrived before we did. Everyone greeted with a hearty, "Merry Christmas," or *"God Jul,"* (Norwegian) or *"Glad Jul,"* (Swedish) and they talked and laughed together. It was a happy time. There were nearly thirty school desks with seats that were occupied by parents with younger children. Others were standing. School age children would present the program.

When it was time to begin, the teacher asked two of the older boys to light the candles on the tree. It was very beautiful! The school children recited their pieces. I felt so proud when my sister Ellen, cousin Bertha and their classmate Ethel Hanson, came from behind a curtain in flowing white robes (sheets) with glittering silver garlands in their hair, and sang a carol. Aunt Sarah, who had never mastered English, said in a loud whisper, *"Dem skal være engeler!"* (They are supposed to be angels!) Several people snickered because she was heard all over the room. After the program, we were given a gift of candy, nuts, and an apple. Then it was time to get all bundled up to face the walk home in the frigid air. Somehow with wonderful memories dancing in our heads, the distance did not seem as long as it was on the way over.

My mother gave a party for the school children during the Christmas holidays, and she invited the teacher too. I know we played many games, but I recall one in particular. My mother explained, "I know all country kids are very familiar with the noise a chicken makes as it lays an egg, but I feel that the boys could do the best job of mimicry." She then placed two kitchen chairs in the middle of the floor and two boys sat facing each other, and cackling away. Oliver Hill did his very best to sound authentic. When he was getting off the chair, Mom quickly slipped an egg onto the chair from behind him. He was so shocked and embarrassed at the sight of the egg that he said, "But how did I do that?"

Mama always tried to be fair with us. One time some company from Duluth visited. As they were leaving, they gave a $2.00 gift to Ingvald. Mom divided it up between us younger children. We each ordered a pair of bedroom slippers with the money. There were other times when money was given to Agnes or me and that, too, was divided in the same fair way.

Every Christmas season, Mom baked some special cookies in shapes of trees, stars and people. We hung them on the tree by putting a needle with thread through them. We also hung up ribbon candies. Often, we noticed a headless or footless cookie man, or half a tree, or even just an empty string hanging on a bough. We knew that Mom wanted us to have them. She enjoyed watching us.

We were so excited when at last it was Christmas Eve. Grandma Kari and Grandpa Erik, and Uncle Krist were with us. Often Uncle Harry and Uncle Joe were invited to supper as well, and would enjoy the whole evening. Grandma helped Mom make *rømmegrøt* (a sweet porridge made with cream). Then there was always *lefse* and *lutefisk*. [I'll explain lutefisk for those who are not Scandinavians. *Lutefisk* is a Cod fish caught off the coast of Norway and preserved by salting and drying the meat. The process for making the fish tender and edible again is a long one, taking nine weeks. It is no wonder it was a once-a-year specialty. First the dried fish is soaked for six weeks in lye water to remove the salt from it. Our mother made her own lye from ashes. Then for an additional three weeks it is soaked in clear water. The flesh is then very tender and flaky. On Christmas Eve it is boiled and eaten with melted butter over it – Yum!!] After the meal was over, we had to wash dishes before we could really begin other festivities. We worked real fast!

When we were ready, the candles were lighted on the tree. Then Mom and Grandma joined hands with us children around the Christmas tree, and we sang *"Gledelig Jul! Hellige Jul!"* ("Silent Night.") After we sang another song or two, Uncle Krist said he would hide in the store where none of us kids could find him. He added, "I need a minute or two so I can find a good spot first." We gave him some time, then when we all went into the store to look for him, Mom closed and latched the door so we could not go back into the living room until she let us in again. We searched and searched but we could not find him. Finally, Mom let us in. Stacks of gifts were all around the tree! To our surprise Uncle Krist was there too! After a year or two, we caught on that Uncle Krist would go out the oil room door. Then, while we were kept out of the way, he helped Dad bring in the presents from some shed where they were hidden. After we did catch on, we never said anything because it was such fun.

We received lots of nice things like paints, crayons, books, games, wind-up toys, horns, or paper dolls. I'll never forget my first doll that said "Mama" when I laid her down. Of course, we usually got some new clothes too, but Dad loved to buy us toys, as did Mom. As we grew older, we received a sled or skis - almost a necessity for country kids in the North Woods.

PHOTO:
Ingvald's
toy car,
1923.

## Chapter 16
## THE ONE-ROOM SCHOOL
### by Helga

For a long time I had looked forward to my first day of school. It was exciting to walk the three-quarters of a mile with Ellen, Karl and Inger, all of us swinging our shiny lunch pails. Our lunches were usually only a sandwich, and maybe a cookie, but not often. Sometimes, it was only bread with Karo Syrup on it – what a sticky mess that was!

Our young school teacher, Miss Payne, was very pleasant and kind. She rang a big bell when it was time for classes to begin. In the room there were four rows of desks with six or seven per row. The students were from eight families: Gilbertson, Persson, Scofield, Hill, Jacobson, Nelson, Hanson and Mattson. There were eight grades, and she had to teach all the classes. I had trouble remembering not to speak Norwegian since that was all we spoke at home. In fact, I had to learn English along with some of the other immigrants' children.

PHOTO: Nass School

At recess, it was fun playing in the schoolyard with so many other children, nearly thirty. When we had arguments, as all children do, we would split into groups of our nationalities: Norwegians and Swedes in one place, Finns in another, and Germans in still another. Each group spoke its own language. All too soon we tired of that, so we quickly forgot our disagreements and played together again.

We usually walked to and from school, but there were times in the winter when we were given a ride. There was a certain German bachelor, who occasionally came to the store. On particularly cold afternoons, if he was there waiting for the mail, our mom would ask if he would drive his pickup to the school and bring the children home, to save them the long cold walk. He was always glad to do it.

In the spring when the snow melted, the water created a bad washout across the entire road where a culvert should have been put in. Water was over a foot deep and was too wide for us younger ones to jump across. Our neighbor, Mr. Hill, the one who had lost three of his children to diphtheria, served as a guardian angel for us. He stood by the water, waiting for all of

PHOTO: Back: Ellen, Karl, Inger
Front: Helga, Agnes

us to come, as we would be walking to school. Then he would carry us piggy-back across to the other side. We really appreciated the kindness of our neighbors.

By the time Agnes and Ingvald started school, Ellen was in the eighth grade, so there were six of us going to the same little school. One day at recess, we were playing and using the water pump as our goal. I had my hand on the open cogs of the pump when a boy began pumping water. My pointer finger was caught between the cogs, cutting it deeply. When I cried out in pain, the boy got frightened and ran away, so I had to call someone else to lift the pump handle to release my finger. I felt sick, but I didn't faint. The teacher wrapped my finger in a handkerchief. I still have a scar.

There was a family living near us who were poorer than any of the rest of us. The children came to school shivering in their rags. The father was mentally ill and often kept the family up all night while he told them stories. The children slept at their desks at school. The teacher was very understanding and encouraged them to rest.

Mom decided to do something to help clothe the children, yet she could not afford to do anything monetarily. She wrote to the Red Cross in Duluth, explaining the situation and giving the ages and sizes of the four school-age children. Not long before Christmas, a big box came from the Red Cross which included everything the children needed in warm clothing, even coats with sheepskin-lining. My mother knew that the poor family would be too proud to accept charity, so she could not give them the box labeled from the Red Cross. She wisely repackaged it, glued on some old canceled stamps, and addressed it to them. On the corner for the return address, she printed the name of their grown son who lived in Washington. She copied the correct address from a letter he had written to his parents.

The children came to school in their nice new clothes and proudly told us that their brother had sent all of it from Washington. Weeks later, one of them said, "We wrote a letter to our brother to thank him, and he wrote back saying he didn't send the box."

My sister told them, "He must have been joking. You don't know anyone else in Washington who could have sent them, do you?" We kept Mom's secret and were happy to see those children wearing the warm clothing.

A public school nurse visited our little one-room school once or twice a year to check each child. We were all very nervous when our name was called because she examined us in front of all the other kids. However, we did not have to disrobe at all. She just checked eyes, ears, teeth, and throats, plus checked scalps for head lice. My exam was fine, but I recalled having had head lice once before. I had traded caps with my friend and then I began scratching. Mom investigated and was greatly perturbed when she found lice. She washed my head with kerosene to get rid of them and she cautioned me, "Never again put on someone else's cap."

One time, the school nurse gave each of us a toothbrush and a small tube of toothpaste and instructed us how to use them. Not one of us had ever owned a toothbrush before this. At recess, Oliver Hill smelled of the toothpaste then tasted it. He licked his chops and proceeded to eat it all! Many of the other boys did the same. It was probably the sweetest thing they had eaten in their whole lives. Some of the kids used to eat paste when we were working with that too. The paste was made from flour and water. Maybe some were really hungry.

As springtime came, we usually ate our lunch outside, but on cold or rainy days we sat at our desks to eat.

One cold day, the teacher heard a roar in the chimney, which was right behind her desk. Suspecting a chimney fire, she called the attention of my elder sister who was seated near the door. "Ellen, will you go out quickly and look up on the roof?"

Ellen jumped to her feet, obeying without question. In a few seconds she was back in the doorway shouting with a tremor of fear in her voice, "The roof is on fire!"

We all felt a sudden panic, but the teacher calmed us as she gave orders, "Boys and girls, gather up your wraps on your way out. Hurry now!" She was being thoughtful of us, knowing we would need our coats out in the chilly air of early spring.

"No pushing! No screaming! Hurry, children!"

Soon we were all outside, fumbling to put on our coats, and watching mesmerized as the flames by this time had engulfed the entire roof.

Then the teacher suddenly gasped. Her hand shot to her mouth as she mumbled, "My purse! My purse is still in there!"

My brother, Karl, then age eleven, was standing close enough to hear. On impulse, he leaped toward the burning building and was inside before the young teacher could realize what was happening. Karl readily found the purse by the teacher's desk, but on his way back out, while glancing up nervously at the inferno overhead, he bumped into the corner of a desk, dislodging the purse from his hand, and sending it sailing to the floor. Instinctively, Karl knew he did not have sufficient time to stoop and pick it up. He gave it one grand kick toward the open door.

Those of us standing outside watching fearfully, saw the purse come flying out the door, followed closely by Karl. Just as he leaped clear of the doorway, there was a thunderous crash of the roof falling in.

The teacher ran to Karl, not only grateful to him for saving her purse, but mainly relieved that he had come out alive. After thanking him, they stood together facing the blaze. The teacher lived in a little room at the rear of the school. It, too, was now being consumed by the intensity of the fire. She may have been thinking of her possessions that were burning, but somehow, as she stole a glance at the face of the brave boy beside her, her losses did not seem so great.

Another one-room school was built that summer. We had to start school in August to make up the weeks we had missed after the fire. There was only tarpaper on the exterior, and it got so hot inside, that it was almost unbearable. Agnes fainted one day and the teacher revived her with cold water at the pump. When others nearly fainted as well, the teacher decided to have some of the classes outdoors until the weather would become cooler.

*   *   *   *

Many children got notices through the mail that they could sell Cloverleaf Salve and they would earn premiums. Karl sold enough to get a little movie machine when he was twelve or thirteen years old. He had to crank it by hand, but he enjoyed showing the film to any neighbor who came by. He only had one film, "Tom Mix." It was a very jerky picture like all the first movies were, but we thought it was really great that we had a movie of our own.

I believe we saw our first movie in Cook in 1929. It was a silent film with words appearing on the screen to explain a situation, or words spoken by an actor or actress. My cousin Anna was the one who sat at the piano and played all through the film.

PHOTO: Cousin Anna Persson

# Chapter 17
## BARE NECESSITIES
### by Helga

One Christmas, Dad gave Mom a second-hand treadle sewing machine. She was delighted and was eager to try it. The old machine she had was in such bad condition that she had given up trying to sew on it. She sewed nearly everything we girls wore, and also made shirts for the boys. In late summer, she would sew up a whole bolt of flannel to make warm nightgowns, slips, and bloomers for the six females in the family.

One time, Dad brought home a bolt of red and white checked gingham material. Poor Mom sewed and sewed! She was so tired of it, she must have had nightmares in red and white for a while after that. She made dresses out of that bolt and trimmed them in white organdy. Only Laura had a different plaid fabric for hers.

PHOTO: Back row: Sanna, Laura and Ellen. Center row: Karl and Inger. Front row: Ingvald, Agnes and Helga.

Mom had a spinning wheel so she would card and spin wool into yarn. There was a constant whirring sound when she was spinning early in the morning. She also sang as she worked. She had a good soprano voice. It was pleasant to wake up to the sound of her singing. Being early, we would often turn over and go back to sleep, lulled by the whirring of the spinning wheel, and the lilting tunes of the Swedish hymns like *"Han Skal Opne Parle Portan"* (He, the Pearly Gates Shall Open.) Mom did a lot of knitting with the wool yarn she spun. She made scarves and mittens for the whole family as well as warm socks for the four males. Sometimes she knitted while visiting with people over the counter in the store. Her hands would not be idle. If she wasn't knitting, she was folding paper to make boats and airplanes, placing them in a neat row on the counter as she talked. We children loved to play with them. As I think of Mom, several verses from Proverbs 31 come to mind.

> *"She seeketh wool, and flax, and worketh willingly with her hand. She layeth her hands to the spindle, and her hands hold the distaff. She is not afraid of the snow for her household: for all her household are clothed with scarlet. She looketh well to the ways of her household, and eateth not the bread of idleness. Her children rise up and call her blessed. A woman that feareth the Lord, she shall be praised."* (Proverbs 31:13, 19, 21, 27, 28a)

It was Mom who saw to it that we had a large garden and potato field every summer. It was a necessity to help feed such a big family. Hoeing the potato patch was hard work and we kids hated that job. If it hadn't rained for a while, the gumbo clay was almost like cement. It might have been easier to do the job with an ax or a pick than with a hoe. Each of us had to do a certain number of rows, according to our ages. We complained a lot, but we did get the work done, and of course Mom was right – it didn't hurt us.

There was always the threat of losing our potato crop to

the orange and black hard-shelled potato bugs. They feasted on the growing plants, and when they became too numerous, they robbed the roots of nourishment. Mom gave us an incentive to help rid the field of those bugs. She would pay us a penny for every hundred bugs we would pick. When I had put 100 bugs in my jar, I would take it to Mom. She would pour boiling water on them to kill them. Then I would go back to pick some more. I was diligent because I had dollar signs - or more likely Lincoln pennies - in front of my eyes. There were two things I really wanted to buy: I felt I badly needed a leather belt for myself, and shoes for my doll. I didn't want her to have cold feet. It was 10 cents for each of those items in the Montgomery Ward catalog. Several days and 2000 bugs later, I had my 20 cents, but I sadly informed Mom, "I can't order the doll shoes after all. Elva already ordered them." I thought there was only one of each item in the catalog and my cousin had beaten me to it. Mom laughed and assured me that the mail-order company had many of each item. I was elated that I could still buy the doll shoes with my hard-earned money.

[Later there was an insecticide called Paris Green. When dusted on the potato plants, there were no more bugs – and no more means for me to make money.]

PHOTO: Ingvald, Agnes, Helga, Inger, Karl.
Helga often carried her doll around.

Inger had no interest in earning money. She did not consider it worth the trouble of handling bugs. One day she went into the store. No one was in there, so when she saw the candy bars in the glass case, she was tempted to take one. Although she knew it was wrong, she reasoned, *the store belongs to our family, so it's not really stealing.* She took a Babe Ruth candy bar out the back of the case and had the wrapper half undone, when the bell over the door rang. A customer had just entered. Quickly Inger folded the wrapper back around the candy bar and slipped it back into the case. Then she made her way around the counter to ask the customer if she could help her with anything.

It took quite a while to help retrieve some things from the shelves, measure or weigh certain items, and wrap the lady's purchases. At last, when the customer was gone, and the store again was empty, Inger skirted back around the counter, eager to retrieve the candy bar from the glass case. Her mouth was watering with the anticipation of the special treat. Her plans were to go out and hide in the corn field where she could sit unseen and eat the Babe Ruth very slowly, savoring each bite. Candy bar in hand, Inger nonchalantly walked out.

When she successfully reached the corn field, she breathed a sigh of relief and proceeded to remove the wrapper. Her joy of anticipation faded as a piece of paper fell out. The little note, written in her mother's handwriting read, "You owe me 500 potato bugs." That candy bar didn't taste as good as Inger thought it would. She did pay her price by collecting the potato bugs, but she wondered all the while how a mother seems to know everything. What she didn't know was that Mom had a peephole from the kitchen, so if she heard the bell, indicating that someone had entered the store, she could look and see who was there. She had seen Inger putting the candy bar back into the case, so while Inger was busy with the customer, her mother had slipped the note into the wrapper. It seems that every child is tempted to steal at some time or another. It is good when the child is caught early. Inger was one who had a conscience about it and was sorry for what she had done. *"For whom the Lord loveth He correcteth."* (Prov.3:12a) In time Inger did give her heart to Jesus and was a faithful, loving Christian all her life.

In the garden Mom had planted more peas than we could use during the summer, knowing that we children would enjoy helping ourselves. She hadn't expressly told us to eat them, probably because she understood human nature that if she told us to eat them, we'd probably avoid them like the plague. As it was, we squatted between the rows and ate to our heart's content. Though we left empty pods, she never mentioned it. There were still plenty of peas to have them with meals throughout the summer.

At that time, it was not known how to home-can vegetables, except for making pickles. Mom made lots of pickled beets, pickled carrots, dill and sweet pickles, tomato relish, and chow chow relish (mostly cabbage.) We had potatoes all winter, but the last of the rutabagas and carrots in the cellar shriveled up to nothing by midwinter. Then, with the exception of pickled ones, there were no more vegetables until summer.

Our meager winter diet was supplemented with as much of the canned berries as we could stand – without tiring of them. Some years the wild strawberries were plentiful, and sometimes it was a good year for raspberries; but mostly we counted on lots of blueberries. We all helped with the picking. Strawberries came first. The wild ones are tiny - as small as a little fingernail - but their flavor is ever so sweet! It was tedious picking to get enough for putting up some jams, and jellies. Raspberries ripened last, in August. Our arms got scratched by the thorns while picking those. Blueberries were the most plentiful and ripened for about six weeks in midsummer. They were bountiful in areas where loggers had cut the timber, then burned the slashing. Dad would drive us to places where we could find the berries. It was usually about fifteen miles from home. He would put a big box in the back of the truck where we could dump our berries every time our pail was full. If we found a patch, we picked until we could not see one ripe berry left. It was good if we could beat the bears to the good patches. One time Laura came around a bush and was face to face with a black bear. They both turned and ran.

We children had to clean all the berries when we got home - that is, getting twigs, stems, leaves, and bugs out of the box. Mom then had the big job. She stood by the hot wood range, perspiring, while pouring boiled blueberry sauce into two-quart jars. (Yes, there were such jars, mostly made of blue glass.) Some days, the outside temperature was over 100 degrees F, but it was hotter inside while canning. She usually canned about 300 quarts each year.

    We seldom had fresh meat except in the fall when we would butcher a hog. It didn't last long when feeding a family of ten - or eleven when Uncle Krist lived with us. We raised a few head of cattle, but we could not afford to butcher our own beef for eating. When we had cows, at least we had milk, cream, and butter for a while. When Dad needed a new tractor, or wanted to trade cars, he would sell the stock to a Jewish cattle buyer. Then we were back to using canned milk in our cereal again – yuck!

    My dad was not a hunter, so we did not have venison like some of the other farmers did – except in later years when Johnny or Karl would shoot a deer. We snared rabbits for meat in winter. At other times, we just did without meat. We could not afford to eat the canned meat off the store shelves either. Since more and more families purchased their own car, they bought most of their groceries in town so the business of our store was not flourishing as in earlier years. On second thought, we did enjoy fresh fried chicken toward fall. Mom always mail-ordered two or three hundred baby chicks early in the spring and when they grew big enough, we feasted on them, though a few of them were kept through the winter as laying hens.

    One year we raised a bull calf that got mean as soon as he was full grown. He was wild-eyed and whenever anyone came near the fence, he would snort and grovel so the dirt would fly. That fence, by the way, was poorly repaired with sticks wherever a post had rotted off, so it was not much of a safeguard against that bull. One day when Dad came home and saw the way that dangerous animal was acting, he said, "I'll teach that animal a lesson so he'll behave." He told Ingvald to go get the shotgun and some fine shot. Ingvald was too young to know what fine shot was, so he got the buckshot instead.

Dad took aim and shot the bull in the chest. He had intended just to sting him, but the bull bellowed and flew up in the air, a big gaping hole in his chest. When he came down, his front legs buckled under him. He staggered to his feet, but then toppled over. It was a hot summer day, but Dad had to get help to butcher the big beast. Dad surely did make that critter behave himself! Mom had to cut the meat into small pieces and put it into jars. She baked it in the oven for hours to can it. Then we did have some meat for a while.

That was not the end of the bull episode. Dad took two of the jars of the canned meat with him when he went to his camp where he was sawing lumber. On the way there, the game warden flashed his lights and stopped him to search for illegal game. He had a new warden with him and was anxious to show off just how this should be done. Finding the jars of canned meat, he opened one to taste it. "Yes, that's venison all right!"

My dad protested, "I've never shot a deer in my life! I just shot a bull and my wife canned the meat."

The know-it-all warden refused to listen, insisting that it was venison, so he took both jars. He said he would send the meat to St. Paul to be tested and that we would get our jars back. We never did hear from that warden again. We got no apology and didn't even get the jars back. Dad did his best to embarrass the cocky warden by writing a letter that was printed in the Open Forum column of the *Hibbing Daily Tribune*. In the letter he said, "The warden threatened to arrest me for those jars of canned beef and that's not bologna!" He warned farmers who might have to shoot a dangerous bull, that they had better watch out, or the game warden might arrest them and confiscate the meat too.

Whenever farmers would discover the remains of a dead calf or sheep, they immediately went out to hunt down the bear that had killed it. One time, our neighbor Gust Hill killed a 500-pound bear. He offered the meat to several different families who each refused it. When he offered it to us, we were glad to get it. It was late in the fall, so it was cold enough that the meat kept well without being canned. We ate and enjoyed it. It especially made good roasts because it was fat like pork.

## Chapter 18
## CHILDHOOD IN THE NORTH WOODS
### by Helga

Our inadequate diet probably contributed to our ill health in winter. We always got the flu around Christmas time and were never very well again until summer. I believe that is why Mom tried to get us to eat as much fresh vegetables as possible in summer.

When Inger was about seven years old, she became very ill. Mom phoned the doctor to come from Cook. He diagnosed the case as scarlet fever. He left the medication for her including some cough medicine, with instructions for Mom to follow so Inger would get well.

Some officials, perhaps from the health department in town, put up a red quarantine sign on our outer bedroom. My mother laughed very hard when she saw the sign. It actually read, "Guaranteed." Both Mom and Inger were isolated for three weeks. Ellen, who was but a twelve-year-old, tended to the store and post office and also took care of the rest of us kids. She did the cooking and brought food to Mom and Inger, too.

When Inger was better, she came out to play and we met her at the swing. She told us she had some delicious cough syrup. Then she brought it out to us so we could each have a spoonful of it. When Mom discovered us enjoying Inger's cough medicine, she got very upset and thought we would all come down with scarlet fever. We didn't get sick, but later Mom noticed our skin peeling and presumed we all may have had a light case of it.

Bad tonsils and adenoids contributed greatly to our ill health too. When we didn't have the flu, we had tonsillitis. Inger's adenoids were so bad she could not breathe through her nose when she was sleeping. One beautiful summer morning when I was 7, Inger 9, and Agnes 6, Dad and Mom took the three of us to Cook to have our tonsils and adenoids removed. We were out-patients. That is, we walked in, had the surgery, and after coming out of the anesthetic, feebly made our way back to the car. The experience I had while being anesthetized was so terrible I hoped I would never have to go through anything like that again. The assistant who held a mask over my face evidently was inexperienced. I heard the doctor telling her not to put so much chloroform on at a time. I didn't go to sleep under the fumes - I simply smothered, unable to breathe. For all three of us, the doctor charged $75. That was a lot of money in 1924.

We started for home over the rough dirt roads, vomiting blood all the way. After we got home, we lay on a blanket out in the sunshine. We were three quiet kids since it hurt to talk. We whispered to Ingvald to bring us some water. He brought us a pan full - as if he thought we were dogs. We had to laugh, even though it hurt to do so. I don't think he was trying to be funny. He was only four years old. He knew we had sore throats. Maybe he thought if we lapped like dogs it wouldn't hurt to swallow. Perhaps he simply didn't want to bring us three glasses of water because he was so busy playing with his wagon.

Ingvald was usually a cheerful child. Of course, like any child, he had his moments. Once, when he was three, and something didn't go his way, he headed down the road on his tricycle, little legs pedaling fast. He was determined to go get the constable to 'set things straight.' He was going in the correct direction, but the constable lived three miles away. Ellen ran after him, bringing him and the tricycle back home.

\* \* \* \*

We had the first washing machine in the Nass area. It had a wooden tub held together with metal bands. Inside the tub was a metal column holding three upside down cups that dashed up and down as well as moving slowly in a circular pattern. It was powered by a little gas engine which Ellen or Mom would start by stepping on a foot pedal. The washer worked well and a big washing was done in a short time compared to the time it took to rub each article on a scrub board. People came over just to see how this marvelous invention worked.

Ironing was a real distasteful job, especially in hot

weather. The wood range had to be pretty hot to heat the flatirons, and if the stove was too hot, the irons would easily scorch the clothes. In later years there was a great improvement when we got a gas iron which kept a consistent temperature.

We took baths in a metal wash tub. In winter, it was beside the pot-bellied stove in the bedroom. The room wasn't very warm. I was always shivering as I got out of the tub. I usually tried to get close to the stove to dry off, but one time I got too close and got burned, or should I say cooked, since I was wet! It was very painful. I couldn't sit down for a couple of weeks. I'm sure I wasn't the only country kid to suffer that experience.

We children always had a certain amount of chores to do. In summer we helped with the gardening. In winter, when days were short, we had the daily job of filling the kerosene lamps and the barn lantern, and washing all the lamp chimneys. There was also lots of wood to carry in for several stoves in the living area as well as in the store. Sometimes we had to split wood too.

No matter what season of the year, we helped clean house. There were always dishes to wash, including the cream separator and the milk pails. There were beds to make, floors to sweep and rugs to shake. One time, I decided to be real helpful by cleaning the bedroom. I made the beds, picked up things, dusted the table, and swept the floor. I took what scraps of waste paper I found and threw them into the pot-bellied stove. Being summertime, the stove had been moved from the center of the room into one corner. When the room was clean, I was very pleased. I planned to tell Mom, so she could see how good it looked, but then I thought of all the scrap paper I had thrown into the stove. I decided to burn that up first. It hadn't occurred to me that since the stove had been moved, its stove pipe chimney was no longer attached. As soon as I lit the match and smoke billowed into the room, I realized what a mistake I had made. Immediately I yelled, "Fire!" Ellen came running from the kitchen with a bucket of water and quickly put out the fire. All was well, but my heart was racing as I thought about how easily I could have burned our whole house down.

I learned to bake bread when I was thirteen. With temperatures at 103F, it was hot indoors too, especially using a wood range. I was proud to show off the beautiful golden loaves I had baked and they tasted even better.

*   *   *   *

In summer, we went out to bring the cows to the barn for milking. I had learned to milk at an early age. We provided a treat in the cows' mangers to entice them into the barn and it usually worked. Mom grew the big mangle beets just for that purpose. We took a few leaves of the beet plant or else Mom would cut up some of the beets for their treat. There were times when it was raining that it was a miserable job to get the cows. We didn't have any rainwear so we simply got wet and cold. The cows would lie down in the wet brush and hide. I think the bell cow must have held her breath so we would not hear one clang of the bell as we went by. When we did find them, we used a switch to get them going toward the barn. Sometimes, they were very cantankerous, as they would suddenly turn and run the opposite direction. There were times I had to give up and go home, wet, shivering and crying with frustration. Then, someone else had to try.

Mostly, cows are a gentle lot, but we had one cow that was very mean. I guess she thought she was a bull. Actually, her calf had been taken away from her, and she blamed any human who happened by. One day, when I was in the pasture, she came after me with that fiery look in her eyes, her head down - ready to get me with her horns. I ran as fast as I could and quickly slipped through the horizontal poles in a big gate just in time to get away from the horns of the cow. However, I came through so fast, with no time to plan where to land, that I fell onto a rusty, dirty manure fork that was laying there on the ground with its tines sticking up. Since my leg was in a bent position, one of the tines got buried in my thigh and two of the others were in my foot.

Somebody ran to get Mom. She held me while Karl pulled with all his strength to pull the fork out of me. I was eight or nine when that happened, so Karl was a husky lad of twelve or thirteen. I was crying, but not so much from the pain, as from fear of having to see the doctor, or possibly the dread of getting a shot. My leg throbbed all night, but I was hoping it would be better by morning. When Mom looked at the wounds the following day, there were two blue lines the length of my leg. She said, "Blood poisoning! We have to take you to the doctor!" Dad was called from the camp where he worked with his saw rig. He came to take me to town. As we passed the school at recess time, I waved to my classmates, wishing I was in school instead. When we got back home, I was kept in bed while Mom applied medicated packs on the puncture wounds, as the doctor had instructed. In two or three weeks, it healed nicely. I never again went into the pasture as long as we still had that mean cow.

Why was I the one who was always getting hurt? One time, I got a big thick sliver so deep in my foot, a doctor had to remove it and dress the wound. I couldn't walk on that foot for a long time. Another time, I was running and stepped on a big rusty nail that was hard to pull out of my foot. Again, I had to go to the doctor. I walked with crutches most of that summer. For that reason everyone called me "Peg leg."

*　*　*　*

When I was nine or ten (1926 or 1927), Dad bought a 32-volt electric light plant with twelve or fifteen special big batteries. He put up a small building away from the house for all the equipment. The light plant itself was mounted on the cement floor and there were long sturdy shelves to hold all the batteries. He kept the door locked at all times except when he was running the light plant. Once a week, the light plant would run all day in order to charge the batteries.

Dad wired the house and store and we were so excited when it was ready for use. We didn't have wall switches, but we turned on a light by a switch right above the naked light bulb. We were taught not to waste electricity, so we didn't use more than one or two lights at a time – except on special occasions like Christmas. When folks came to the store or post office, they were impressed when they noticed that we had electric lights.

There were a lot of flies during hot weather. At first, there weren't any effective ways to get rid of them except with a swatter – and that's not at all effective when children run in and out all day. Something new came on the market that looked like black paper, but it was placed on a plate with vinegar and sugar and it did kill flies! (Well, maybe the flies that died there were diabetic and they just ate too much sugar.) Then someone invented a sticky paper to place on a plate. On a hot day, it had the consistency of Karo Syrup. The flies got stuck and died. One day, Mom and Ellen were in a dither, cleaning the house because they were hosting the Lutheran Ladies' Aid. Mom had put the plate of fly paper on top of a high wardrobe in the bedroom. When the ladies arrived, including Reverend and Mrs. Fadum, no one saw where the preacher placed his hat. When it was time for them all to leave, the preacher reached up to retrieve his hat from the top of the wardrobe. Sheets of sticky goo were dripping from that expensive black hat, as he had placed it right into the plate of sticky flypaper!

Our Lutheran pastor lived in Cook and had his main church pastorate there, but one Sunday a month he made a circuit to preach at Celina, Bear River, ten miles to the southwest of us, and Silverdale, ten miles to the north. We were expected to be present at the worship service at Celina.

Celina Lutheran Church

Bear River Lutheran Church

I first learned about God and faith through my mother, and my grandmother Kari. Then as we attended church, my knowledge about the Bible steadily grew. If Dad was home when the Celina Lutheran Church was having their monthly meeting, we would go there. Sometimes Reverend Fadum would preach in Norwegian and other times he would use English. When I was little I didn't understand the English since we only spoke Norwegian at home. Everyone felt his sermons in Norwegian were better. Of course Norwegian was our heart language, it's no wonder we preferred that. Fadum did have a tender heart and often got teary when he preached.

PHOTO: Missionary Ladies with Northern Gospel Mission

Whenever Dad was away from home with his portable saw rig and was not around on a Sunday, Mom would let us walk to the mission chapel instead. Northern Gospel Mission had mission stations throughout the North Woods and they sent the missionaries there to reach out to the community of immigrants. Sometimes their stations were run by a young couple or a family; other times there were single missionary ladies. It was half the distance for us to walk through the woods to the mission chapel, instead of going the three miles to Celina. We much preferred going to the chapel. Mom's faith and trust in Jesus was very real and personal, so she also wanted us to know the Lord. We loved to go to Sunday School at the mission. The singing was lively and uplifting and the Gospel message was clearly taught.

One year, Miss Etter and Miss Regeir were the missionaries. We liked them, especially Miss Regeir who was young, pretty, and full of pep. Once a week the two ladies would come to Nass to practice songs for Sunday. We had a pump organ. It was old and wobbly, but Ellen could play it. One of the times they came was on March 31. My mother just happened to know that it was Miss Regeir's birthday. While everyone gathered around the organ to sing, Mom surprised them by setting a small gift and a cake on the table for Miss Regeir. The lady, obviously touched that her birthday was remembered, showed great delight. I felt special as well since I shared the same birthday with this dear lady.

Each summer, we walked to the missionaries' cabin to attend Daily Vacation Bible School. It always went for two weeks. On the year when Miss Etter and Miss Regeir were there, we enjoyed the singing and the Bible stories so much that we begged the ladies to extend the VBS for a third week. They gladly did so. We memorized a lot of Scripture, not only during VBS, but also in Sunday School. Many of those verses, or chapters are still with me today.

After Miss Etter and Miss Regeir left, the mission station was moved farther north. Then it was over three miles for us to walk to attend church, or summer's Daily Vacation Bible School. One summer, the walk was so hot that we all arrived very tired and thirsty. The missionaries had prepared cherry flavored Kool-Aid, an expensive treat that country families could never afford – five cents per packet, which made two quarts. It sure tasted good.

At times, there were special nightly preaching services in the

PHOTO: Coming home from a church service. Sanna, with Helga, Ingvald, Agnes, Karl, and Inger.

mission chapel. On those brisk October evenings, I recall walking beneath a star-studded sky to the chapel. Aunt Sarah and Mom led the way, one of them carrying a lantern, as we made the trek through the woods.

With the exception of walking to church, we generally went barefoot in summer. We children thought it was great to shed our shoes as soon as the weather was warm enough, because all the kids did it. The truth was, we couldn't afford to be wearing out our shoes in summer.

We were fortunate to get shoes in time for school in the fall. I remember at age eight or nine being so excited when I received a new pair of shoes that I was eager to show them to Uncle Andrew. With shoes in hand, I ran across the meadow to the Persson homestead. Reaching their cabin, I found the door ajar, so I didn't knock. I quietly slipped inside, but then stopped abruptly. Uncle Andrew was busy talking with my mother. They both had tears. Momentarily I stood still, fearful that something was wrong. Then I realized their tears were tears of joy. Uncle Andrew was sharing that he had been to the mission chapel and had accepted Jesus into his heart. He was overjoyed to know that his sins had been forgiven. I stood there quietly in the doorway, a smile slowly replacing my apprehension. I perceived that this very special moment did not need to be shattered by my interruption. Slowly tucking my shoes behind my back, I slipped out the door. I could show off my new shoes some other day.

## Chapter 19
## ENTERTAINING OURSELVES
### by Helga

Nothing much happened in the country in the way of entertainment. Therefore, it stirred up a lot of excitement, at least among us children, when a circus came to Nass. I called it a circus for lack of a more appropriate term, because it didn't begin to compare with the Big Top, the three-ring circus of today.

There was a bear on a chain, a few monkeys, dogs and ponies. There was no big tent - only benches set up in a circle for audience seating. I'm not sure what the admission was, but I presume 10 cents for children and 25 cents for adults. I remember watching the ponies trotting around in a circle while trained dogs and monkeys climbed a ladder to jump on the backs of the ponies to ride. It was all very orderly – each hitchhiker knew when it was his turn and just how many rounds he could ride before he was to jump off so another rider could get on.

\* \* \* \*

When we were quite small, Uncle Krist took us swimming on hot days. He had bought bathing suits - the correct term for those days - for each one in the family. They were one-piece with a top that looked like a man's undershirt - or a tank top - and the overskirt was slit on both sides. They were navy with white trim. They were so much more comfortable than wet clothes! We walked to the meadow where a stream bubbled along on its way to the pond. We were not permitted to go to the pond, but we could splash in the stream as long as we liked. It was not deep. One time Mom came to the meadow with us. She stuck her big toe into the water and said, "Brr! That's too cold!" She turned right around and went back home.

\* \* \* \*

Sometimes I played with my sisters, or with our cousins. Inger and cousin Elva liked to play house. Inger and Elva were the older ones, so Agnes and I had to play the part of being the children in the family. Sometimes mud pies were made for make-believe food. At other times the scraps at the bottom of the candy barrel in the store were used. One would think we would love the candy, but we certainly did not. Inger would stir the candy bits into water and serve it to us as "soup." It was syrupy sweet and a slimy goo. That's when I quit playing house and decided to play with my brother Ingvald instead.

PHOTO 1916: Playhouse. Left to Right: Ellen, Laura, Karl, Johnny, Sanna with Inger on her lap, and Cousin Anna.

Ingvald and I always had fun together. I was a tomboy. One day, he thought it would be fun to climb to the top of a spruce tree and swing as the tree would lean. He went up first, and as he neared the top he swung in a circular motion. It looked fun, so I decided to try it too, but I was three years older and was chunky besides. The tree broke and I fell six feet down, landing on my back on the corner of a big packing crate, knocking the wind out of me. That episode wasn't much fun. It was a painful experience for those seconds or minutes that I couldn't breathe. It seemed as if I never would get my breath back.

Another time, we were climbing trees near the barn and there was a haystack nearby to jump into. Well, I didn't realize that the woodpeckers had damaged my tree and when I added my weight to the weakened tree, it broke suddenly and I fell flat on my back on the ground and had the wind knocked out of me again! While I lay there struggling for breath, Ingvald saw what happened from his perch in another tree. He jumped out of his tree and landed in the haystack to come and see if I was all right. It struck me so funny to see him sailing through the air with boots several sizes too big for him, that when I got my first gasping breath, I laughed.

Empty 55-gallon drums also provided some fun. Laying each drum on its side, we would balance as we walked on them to make them roll. Ingvald would say, "Follow me" and we'd start down the hill to the barn, each on his own 'vehicle.' When Ingvald couldn't quite make it to the top of a hump, he'd come rolling backward and crash into my barrel, so we'd both fly off. We had a lot of laughs. Even though we got a few bumps and bruises, we had barrels of fun.

Some of the teens in the area came to the store on their bicycles. Cousin Hilding rode over quite regularly on his bike to socialize with Karl, the Hill boys, and others. Some of my older siblings also knew how to ride. No one took the time to teach me, but it didn't look that hard to do, so one day, I decided to try it. I thought if I started at the top of a hill, it would be easy. I wouldn't have to pedal so hard to keep up the momentum. I managed to get on and start it rolling, but, naturally I didn't go far before I took a nasty fall and badly skinned my knees. Ellen had compassion when I limped into the house. She cleaned and bandaged my wounds. After my sores were scabbed over, I thought I should be courageous and get back on that bike to conquer it, but, I only managed a repeat performance of my first ride. Again my knees, as well as my hands and an elbow were bleeding after I hit the gravel road. My two failed attempts discouraged me. I never did learn how to ride a bicycle.

Nearly every country kid raised a pet crow by robbing a nest of young ones, so we did too. As he grew older, he flew along and went wherever we went to play, but he became a real nuisance. At times, he pulled the clothes pins - not the spring type - off the clothes on the line, so the wet clothes fell to the ground, or sometimes into mud. We kids got the blame even though we insisted that we were innocent.

One time, Dad took his gloves off to work on some machinery. When he finished the job, he could not find his gloves. Again, we kids were suspect. There were a number of times that small articles mysteriously disappeared. Then, one day, Ellen saw the crow sitting on the clothesline, tugging away until he got a clothes pin off. Then he flew away with it, leaving a piece of wet laundry on the ground. At another time, Dad was getting some lumber off a pile. There were his missing gloves, clothes pins, various nuts, bolts, nails, staples and buttons, tucked between the layers of lumber where the crow had stashed all his loot.

On one occasion, Ellen was out on the porch scrubbing some new potatoes with a metal brush. The gleam of the shiny bristles must have caught the eye of the nosey crow. He watched her until she put the brush down, then he stole it and flew away with it. Ingvald gave chase, but as he kept an eye on the crow which was flying just out of reach in front of him, he fell over a log. It knocked the wind out of him. The crow immediately flew down to the ground, standing just out of reach, his shoe button eyes blinking, waiting patiently for Ingvald to resume the chase. I don't know if we ever did get that brush back.

Our neighbors had a crow too. One day, Mrs. Hill was weeding her strawberry patch. The silent crow stood by, watching her as she pulled weeds and stacked them in a pile. She was nearly finished when she went to the house for a drink of water. Upon her return, the crow had pulled up all the strawberry plants and put them neatly in a pile.

*   *   *   *

I enjoyed picking flowers in the spring. Before all the snow was gone, the white snowdrops appeared and next were buttercups and violets. Wild roses and the state flower, the lady's-slipper, were the prettiest flowers. I liked to pick the delicate pink or white Mayflowers and place them into a little paper basket I had glued together. I would leave it on Mom's desk in the post office while she was out of the room, and then I'd run out to play.

Mom loved flowers. Each year she would plant various types beside the vegetable garden so she could enjoy them while weeding the garden. She usually planted lots of poppies, bachelor buttons, cosmos, zinnias, and nasturtiums. She also planted morning glories by our door with strings for them to climb on. What a fitting name for those flowers. They truly did make the morning glorious, covering that ugly black wall with their smiling faces!

We had what we called a park at the side of the house where the door was. The lawn was kept mowed in that area where we had a picnic table under the pines. Mom planted flowers in an open space where they got plenty of sun: California poppies, forget-me-nots, larkspur, petunias, and tiny fragrant mignonette for edging. There were also some big bushes of golden glow, and several lilacs that were beautiful and fragrant when they bloomed in June.

The tarpaper building was unbearably hot in summer, so we ate out at the picnic table all the time even though the food was cooked inside. Often, we just had salt pork and crackers at noon. The butter dish was always like a pool of water since we had no kind of refrigeration. While Uncle Krist lived with us, he used to put up ice from the pond in the meadow. The ice was placed between layers of sawdust in the ice house. It was a pity that we never had an icebox for summer use, but we did use the ice to make ice cream on special days like the Fourth of July. Occasionally, we went to a lake on that holiday, and we kids would spend many hours swimming.

Dad always brought home cases of pop for July 4th. He treated any neighbor who hap-

PHOTO: Fun at a lake on July 4th.

pened by, as well as letting us have all we wanted. He also spent a lot of money on fireworks which included plenty of little firecrackers and sparklers for us kids. We set out a big flag, and we even had small flags on our car. Cars that went by were also well decorated with flags. In the evening, people would come from miles around to celebrate Independence Day together by watching the fireworks display. One time, Dad bought close to $200 worth, because he enjoyed entertaining friends and neighbors. Mom would rather have spent the money for warm winter clothing, but she knew it wouldn't do any good to say so. It was a glorious display of roman candles, rockets, etc, that filled the night sky with sprays of sparks and stars of every color bursting in midair and falling earthward. In a little more than an hour, $200 had literally gone up in smoke, though we could ill afford it.

*   *   *   *

Uncle Krist enjoyed providing a treat for us kids now and then. He would buy several boxes of Cracker Jacks, open them, and scatter their contents all over the table. Then he would call, "Come chick, chick, chick!" Of course, we knew how to play the game. We had to hold our hands behind our backs and bend to eat our treat just as a chicken pecks away. It was as much fun for him as it was for us.

There was one thing about Uncle Krist that was very aggravating. He would wake up early in the morning and holler at the top of his lungs, "Daylight in the swamp! Daylight in the swamp! Time to get up!" Then he would laugh at our reactions. If we hadn't been so loaded down with covers, we might have hit the ceiling. Nothing made me feel more grumpy than that hair-raising awakening!

If I awoke early and others were still asleep, I really liked to slip out with our hymn book. Then I would go to the swing which was suspended from a beam beside the barn. There I would sing and sing all by myself. I flipped page after page in my morning praise to the Lord. If I didn't know the tune to some particular hymn, I would spontaneously make up my own melody to the words. All too soon, others were rousing and my morning songfest would draw to a close.

One summer Dad built a new barn. We had fun playing hide and seek while the building was under construction. One day, I climbed over the horse stall and expected to slide down the other side to the floor. I didn't know someone had put a huge nail there and it caught the seat of my new overalls. I hung there suspended between the ceiling and the floor. I had to yell for help. When everyone came running, they laughed at the sight of me hanging on the wall. I wasn't hurt, so I was laughing as hard as anybody else.

PHOTO: Helga, Karl, Agnes, Johnny, Ellen holding Ingvald, and Inger.

In winter we loved playing in the snow. Unlike the earlier years when they didn't have proper water-resistant footwear, we children had boots, so we seldom stayed in the house. If I took my doll with me outside, I made sure to bundle her up real good so she wouldn't get cold. Sledding was the most fun. We especially enjoyed it when snow was *"skara"* (crusted over). Then we could run on top, right over fences or bushes. If someone hit a soft place and fell into deeper snow and had to struggle to get back on top, there was much laughter.

On bitterly cold days when we had to stay inside, we played with matches. That's not as bad as it sounds, however. Being country kids, we had been taught the proper use of matches and we respected the element of danger involved when using them. We knew how to build a fire in the stove, but we did not play with matches by lighting them. We used matches (with parental consent) as playing pieces for a game with a top which Dad had carved for us out of wood. The top was square but it came to a point on the bottom and had a little handle on the top. On each side was a letter which stood for a Norwegian word, which directed the moves in the game. The letters were as follows:

    I = *Ingenting* "nothing" – The player had to pass.
    P = *Putte* "Put" – The player had to put three matches onto the game pile.
    H = *Halv* "half" – The player earned half the game pile.
    A = *Alt* "All" - The player earned all of the game pile.

We began the game with ten matches apiece and placed ten on the game pile in the center. Then, each took a turn at spinning the top and when it stopped, the player had to do what the letter indicated. When someone spun an A and depleted the pile in the center of the table, it was replenished with ten more matches out of the match box. Sometimes, a player had to drop out if he ran out of matches. Others then continued playing until the match box was empty. The one with the most matches won the game.

                  \*      \*      \*      \*

    Whether we got in a spat while playing, or if we were being disobedient, my parents practiced discipline. One time I got into a verbal battle with Agnes that I soon regretted. In anger, I grabbed her glass cupie doll. Dad had recently brought them for us from town. I smashed that doll on the bedstead so it broke into a thousand pieces. Mom then took my doll and told Agnes, "Here, now Helga's doll is yours." It was a worse punishment for me to lose my doll than if I had been given a whipping, but it taught me a valuable lesson.

    Mom had a switch - a branch with all the leaves removed, which was kept behind the mirror over the washbowl. She was quick to use it whenever she deemed it necessary. One day, Ingvald decided to dispose of it so she wouldn't be able to administer punishment any more. When Mom found it missing, she must have known who would do that. She made Ingvald go get another one, then he got the first whipping with the new switch. Through discipline, our parents were demonstrating their love to us. *"He that spareth his rod hateth his son: but he that loveth him chasteneth him betimes [promptly]."* (Prov. 13:24)

* * * *

Music also was our entertainment. In 1925, Dad bought our first radio. It was a rather large box of fine varnished wood with a big horn standing on top for a speaker. There were three tuning dials and earphones could be used while tuning or listening. All three dials had to be tuned just right in order to bring in a program. Many times, the only sounds we could get were a lot of squealing and squawking noises that hurt the ears. However, I remember Grandma Kari and Grandpa Erik coming over on Sunday mornings to listen to a church service.

Even without the radio or the old Edison Victrola on which we played cylindrical recordings, we did have music of our own for entertainment. My dad played the violin and Ellen was very good at chording on the pump organ. Ellen could play "Listen to the Mockingbird" more beautifully on that wheezy old foot-pedal organ than I have heard since then. Dad liked to play "Red Wing" as well as lively polkas from the old country. Then too, we would all gather around the organ and sing hymns or old folk songs. Eventually, four of us sisters formed a quartet. Agnes sang tenor, Ellen sang alto, Inger sang bass, and I sang soprano. Mom in particular enjoyed listening to us as we sang. While in our teens we sang for services at the little mission chapel.

PHOTO: Quartet Agnes, Ellen, Inger, Helga

Chapter 20
A NEW SCHOOL
by Helga

After our one-room school burned down, we began hearing talk of closing the small schools and consolidating. Finally in the fall of 1927 when I was in fifth grade, it happened.

The two-story brick building was completed at Togo, six miles from our home. Five buses transported the approximate 100 students to the school. There were more than twenty on our bus. It was blue and white so we named it "The Blue Goose."

PHOTO: Togo School

When we arrived at the school that first day, there were two boys on the front steps. One was running up and down the steps as if he couldn't possibly be still for one minute. That was the first time I remember setting eyes on Edward Rostvit. I never dreamed then that he was to become my life mate! It turned out that he was my age, ten, and was in my fifth-grade class. He remembered seeing me when he and I were seven years old. At that time my dad was driving over to the Rostvit homestead to talk with them about cutting some lumber for them with his saw rig. Agnes and I had ridden along. We were seated in the back of Dad's Model T pickup with our backs against the cab. When Edward saw us he remembered thinking, *now there are a couple of good looking girls!*

The school had four classrooms, with one teacher to each two grades. There was a nice library with lots of books we could

PHOTO: Edward Rostvit (on right) with older brothers Elof and Paul

check out. Next to that, was a big lunchroom which seated all the students and faculty. Each student was assigned a week at a time to either help with the cooking or else to wash dishes and do the cleanup work. We didn't have full meals, but we did have something hot to go with the sandwiches we each brought from home. I remember having vegetable soup, tomato soup, or cocoa.

The indoor toilets were something new to us country kids. There were also washbowls with hot and cold running water – even paper towels for wiping our hands! Every student was required to take a shower once a week. We had to bring our own towel on the day assigned to us. Five or six of us girls were grouped to go into the shower at the same time, under two shower heads. I didn't have to worry about burning my behind on the pot-bellied stove at home any more! On the day that boys were to shower, many of them "conveniently" forgot to bring a towel, so they wouldn't have to bathe.

In the school's basement was a gymnasium for programs, for basketball games, or for playing indoors when the weather was bitter cold. We had periodic fire drills to be sure we could quickly vacate the building in an orderly manner in case of fire. The principal, Mr. Anderson, was timing us. It usually took less than three minutes.

The principal was very strict. We had been told we were never to run in the school building. One time I had a very sore foot. It was a struggle to make it up the long staircase. When I was reaching the top, I hopped up the final step, relieved to have made it. Mr. Anderson saw me make that last triumphant hop. Assuming I had run up the steps, he barked out orders, "Go all the way back down and come up the staircase slowly like you're supposed to!" I knew he would not accept any explanation, so I made the painful descent and came back up again.

Edward Rostvit turned out to be a tease on the playground. On one occasion he took my hat and ran away with it. Another boy grabbed it from him then tossed it from one boy to another. In the process they accidentally tore off a beaded decoration on it. Edward finally got the hat back and returned it to me. We were able to sew the decoration back on it but I did feel badly about my new blue hat. After that, I began to find a candy bar or a package of gum in my desk from time to time. Along with the gifts, there was often a tack on my seat, too. All the girls had to get smart and look before sitting down because it was a favorite pastime of the boys to put tacks on seats and listen for a scream or a gasp as the girl would jump up. I knew the candy, and probably the tacks as well, came from Edward. I admit I liked it.

Our bus was made of a Model T chassis with a big body wired to it. (That's what the adults were saying – that it was not well constructed.) In the spring of that first year at Togo School, we had some very bad rough roads. Roads were gravel and when the snow and ice began to melt, the bus would make zig-zag ruts that would be a foot or so deep. In the mornings, the ruts would be frozen solid and it seemed that we were compelled to zig-zag in the ruts of the previous day.

Apparently, the Model T wheels with the wooden spokes couldn't take that strain. We heard a loud crack as we were coming down a steep hill but we kept going a couple miles after that. I was reading a book when there was a sudden violent jolt that made my head hit against the window frame. The blow on my head dazed me and everything that happened after that seemed unreal. It was like a nightmare to see kids from the other side of the bus coming down at me, as though diving into a swimming pool, I thought. The wheel had broken and the bus was rolling over on its side into the ditch.

 Some of the panicked students were frantically searching for their lunch pails as if that were a matter of life and death. They seemed unaware that they were trampling on others of us who were lying in a mess of broken glass, twisted metal, ice chunks and ice water in the ditch. In my semiconscious state, I could not move but I wondered how long I could live without a breath. It hurt so much to be trampled! The bus driver started shouting at everybody to climb out through the broken rear window. I had no strength to get up, but the bus driver helped me. I was the last one out of the bus. The cold air revived me. No one was killed or even seriously injured. One little boy was hopping around on one foot and exclaiming, "My leg is broken! My leg is broken!" We noticed that he first hopped on one foot and then on the other. He didn't seem to be badly hurt but perhaps he had been trampled on or bruised.

 One of the other school buses came along and the driver offered help. Some of the kids on that bus were crying when they saw what had happened to us. Most of the children from our bus got into the other bus and went on to school. I had wondered why the lid of my dinner pail was full of blood and whose it was. It was my own from a puncture wound in my neck. Agnes' ear was cut so it was drooping over. A car came to take us home. We agreed with each other to smile so we would not give Mom too much of a shock, but she could plainly see that something was wrong. Mom washed off the blood though she couldn't get all the blood out of my hair. She helped us get into dry, clean clothes so the driver could take us to Cook for treatment. Agnes had to have three stitches in her ear. The doctor took quite a while to clean out the puncture wound in my neck and head. He had to dig out bits of gravel and broken glass before he could put in a stitch. He told me, "This will probably hurt. Just step on my foot if it does." I kept stepping on his toes, but he ignored it and kept on working. I guess he thought he at least gave me something to do to get my mind off the pain. Of that full busload, it was amazing no one even got a broken bone! Agnes and I were the only two who needed to see a doctor.

I was nervous and did not sleep well for a long time after that. I would have nightmares and wake up in a cold sweat, gasping for breath as I relived the experience of smothering when I was being trampled. Until the roads improved, I was a nervous wreck on the way to and from school, fearing we would have another accident.

Agnes had other after effects. She came down with pleurisy and had to stay in bed for two weeks. That ice water bath in the ditch was taking its toll.

I would have four years of studies at the Togo School – through eighth grade.

\* \* \* \*

In summers, Ingvald and I worked as hard as any man in the hayfield, especially from the time Ingvald was eleven and I was thirteen. We hand raked hay into windrows with big wooden rakes that had long wooden teeth. Then, we made hay cocks out of them and pitched them up onto the hay wagon. We later pitched it onto haystacks or into the hay barn.

There was a lot of rain one year and before we could put the hay up in the barn, bees had made a hive in a hay cock. When we got on either side of the hay cock and stuck our forks into it, the angry bees attacked us with fierce vengeance! Our faces and arms were covered with red welts from the bee stings.

One summer, my brothers were mowing the hay. We girls carried a pot of coffee, sandwiches and cookies half a mile to the field so our brothers could have afternoon lunch. Our dog was with us. He chased up a mouse that bit him in the tongue and hung there. The dog yipped and tossed his head from side to side until the mouse finally let go and went flying. On the way home, the dog acted very strangely.

When we got home, Aunt Sarah was visiting so we all sat on the beds, talking and laughing. Suddenly, we heard steady thumping under the bed. The dog was on his back, frothing at the mouth and convulsing. We hurried out of the room and closed the door just in time. The dog was bug-eyed and ran around and around the room, barking wildly. We tried to talk to him through the screened window but he didn't hear or see us. Apparently, he got rabies from the mouse that bit him. My brother had to shoot the dog.

* * * *

In 1929 the Depression began. We who lived in the country and had our own gardens, had it better than numerous city folk who couldn't find work to feed their families, and who had to stand in long lines to get a bowl of soup.

My folks were subscribers of the *Duluth Herald* as far back as I can recall. They read about the Depression, but we kids liked the comic strips, especially Little Orphan Annie, Bringing Up Father (Maggie and Jiggs), Blondie, Dick Tracy, and The Katzenjammer Kids. The newspaper included a page just for children and called it The Fair Play Club. They encouraged boys and girls to become members by sending in a drawing, poem, or story. There was a $1.00 prize for the best one published in each of the three categories every day. The next best ones were not awarded any prize but were published under HONORABLE MENTION. I was overjoyed when I won the prize and saw my first poem in print on the Fair Play Club page. This is it:

SPRING

Winter is gone and spring is here;
Now let's forget every worry and fear.
The sun shines brightly; the skies are azure blue;
Soon, we'll find daisies and violets too.
We'll go to the meadow and play by the brook;
We'll climb trees and rest in the shady nook.

That was in 1929, when I was twelve years old. Within two years, seven of my poems were published under HONORABLE MENTION and I won first place again on a second poem, also entitled SPRING, written in 1931. After all, there wasn't much to write about in our dull little corner of the world!

## SPRING

Spring came into the woods today,
She was dressed in colors bright and gay;
She wore a long green silken gown,
From her head, the golden curls hung down.
She's the most beautiful maiden I've seen,
When with flowers she's laden and leaves so green;
She put a green carpet down on the floor,
In place of the brown one that was there before.

When I was fourteen, in 1931, I graduated from eighth grade at Togo School. Our school picnic was at Side Lake that year and the graduation ceremony was performed there in a meeting hall. There were nine of us graduates, including Edward Rostvit. We girls wore white dresses for the occasion. Edward wrote in my autograph book, "When you get married and live by a lake, give me a piece of your (my) wedding cake." Crossing out the word 'your,' he replaced it with 'my.' All our classmates knew we liked each other.

That June, my sister Laura married Paul Rostvit. He was a tall good-looking man with dark curly hair, an older brother of Edward's. We often went to visit them. Since they were living on the Rostvit homestead I would also see Edward. One time, he was eager to show me that he had acquired a car – or what there was of it. It was little more than a chassis with a steering wheel, but it worked. His brother, Paul, had purchased an old man's cabin and this junked car came with it. Paul said, "Edward if you'll buy a battery I need, I'll give you this car." So, for $3.98 he received that hunk of metal with four wheels.

"Want to go for a ride?" he asked, with a hand gesturing toward his machine. It mattered not to me that he didn't have a fancy car - being with him made me happy.

"Sure," I responded with enthusiasm. I looked hesitant as to where I should sit. There was no seat, just the exposed gas tank.

Edward took a cloth and placed it on the tank. "There you

PHOTO: Laura and Paul at the Rostvit
Homestead beside their '29 Model A.

are. There's room for both of us. You can sit here beside me."

He had first driven tractors at age eight. He could drive a Model T shortly after that, and a stick-shift car by the time he was eleven. Now at age fourteen, Edward was thrilled to have a "car" he could call his own. We had fun riding around on the Rostvit farm.

That summer Ellen had a job in Hibbing. Johnny, Karl, and Inger were away, working at the saw mill. Our family was getting smaller – only three kids at home, I being the eldest.

Togo School added two years of high school, but I did not return to school that September. Mom wasn't feeling well and she needed a lot of help so she did not urge me to go back to school. We were milking fourteen cows at that time so I milked half of them while Mom did the rest. In Minnesota, cows are kept in the barn most of the winter so there is lots of work to clean the barn, and to feed and water the stock. If the weather wasn't too bitter, we turned the cows out so they could go to the pond to drink. Mom would chop a hole in the ice, and cover the hole with some old carpets, yet it could still refreeze about six inches overnight.

Meanwhile, if Ingvald wasn't in school, he and I would clean the barn, putting fresh bedding in the stalls. Then we would get hay off the stack and fill the mangers. If the weather was too cold (30-40 below zero) we didn't let the cows out. Then, we would have to carry water into the barn for them. We had a hand-operated windlass to help bring up each pail of water. That was a lot more work than letting the cows drink at the pond!

Winters were long with much snow and bitter cold weather. Because of being so far north – seventy miles from the Canadian border – we saw the phenomenon, aurora borealis, or as it is commonly called 'northern lights.' On cold clear nights the lights ripple and flash across the northern horizon in a spectacular display.

PHOTO: Gilbertsons visit the Rostvits. Back: Eida R, Inger G, Paul and Laura R, Gunda R. Front: Ingvald, Agnes, and Helga G, and Edward R. Do I look happy to be near Edward? We were age 13.

## Chapter 21
## A CHANGE WITHIN
By Helga, then Ellen

For everyone, life takes different turns. One may think he is in control of his own destiny, yet if honestly considered, there are many things in life over which we have little or no control. Even unexpected circumstances can change the entire direction of one's life. *"A man's heart deviseth his way: but the Lord directeth his steps."* (Prov. 16:9). God is sovereign, yet loving. He is patient *"...not willing that any should perish, but that all should come to repentance."* (II Peter 3:9). We are glad that each one in our family at one point or another, turned toward God. Here are the stories of three of us siblings and how the "change of heart" took place.

**LAURA AND PAUL'S STORY**

When my sister Laura married Paul Rostvit, he was not a Christian man. It was the days of prohibition and Paul's father, Ole, had been making and selling moonshine. Paul illegally transported the liquor to Canada. He was also drinking the moonshine (whiskey) and the home-brew (beer) that they made. On Saturday nights he often went to the Bearville Township's hall, where he and his buddies got together to smoke, drink, and play cards. All of this greatly saddened the heart of Paul's mother, Anne. She loved the Lord and prayed that her family would come to faith in Christ.

Within months of Paul and Laura's wedding, news spread through the area that for two weeks there would be an evangelistic preaching meeting held in the Bearville Town Hall. Vernon Gaudy would be conducting the meeting with Reverend Cook doing the preaching. The meeting hall was near the

Rostvit's homestead.

When Paul's two drinking buddies learned about the meeting, they knew the hall would not be available for their usual Saturday night fun. Then one of the guys said, "I know what to do. Let's go to the meeting and cause a disturbance. It would be fun to break it up."

"Yeah, let's do it," chimed in the other man. "Can't you just imagine the look on the face of the 'hellfire brimstone preacher' when we scatter the crowd?"

The other piped in again, "How about doing it on the last night? We can sit in the back, then, make all our commotion right near the end of the meeting. We'll be the grand finale! Ha! Ha!"

Paul watched with amusement as his two buddies bantered about their plans. Then they turned to Paul. "We can work out the details of what we'll do. What do you think, Paul? Are you in?"

Paul shrugged his shoulders, "I suppose," he complied.

The meeting hall was packed each night for the preaching services. Finally, the last night came. Paul and his wife, Laura, entered and took their seats near the rear. Paul glanced back to see his two buddies seated in the back row. The meeting started with congregational singing, then came the preaching. Paul had fully intended to join his buddies and disrupt the meeting – but God had different plans. As Paul and Laura listened to the preaching, their hearts were moved. It was as if the evangelist was preaching personally to them. Paul thought on his life. He was striving to make money – even illegally – and was just living to please himself. He was being convicted about his sin. Between his own thoughts, he was hearing snatches of what the pastor was saying, *"While we were yet sinners, Christ died for us...For the wages of sin is death; but the gift of God is eternal life through Jesus Christ our Lord."*

Laura was feeling the same conviction in her heart.

*"How shall we escape if we neglect so great salvation..."* God was drawing the young couple to Himself. At the close of the sermon, a hymn was sung as Rev. Cook extended an invitation, "If you want to be saved, come to the front and make it publicly known that you are surrendering your heart to Jesus."

Paul and Laura both stepped out of their row and walked down the aisle.

Paul's buddies gawked, eyes wide with disbelief. One of them nudged the other and spoke in a hoarse whisper, "Let's get out of here before this religion hits us too!" They didn't wait around, but high-tailed it out the door.

As for Paul, his lifestyle changed dramatically. There was no more drinking liquor, nor making and selling moonshine, and no more smoking, nor meeting with his former buddies to play cards. He did try to influence them for Christ, but he was no longer their steady friend. *"Blessed is the man that walketh not in the counsel of the ungodly, nor standeth in the way of sinners, nor sitteth in the seat of the scornful. But his delight is in the law of the Lord; and in His law doth he meditate day and night,"* (Psalm 1:1,2). Now at the breakfast table Paul and Laura would open God's Word, reading a passage of Scripture and praying together. He would often be heard to say, *"This is the day which the Lord hath made; we will rejoice and be glad in it,"* (Psalm 118:24). Laura, too, always demonstrated a gentle and loving Christ-like spirit.

*   *   *   *

## HELGA'S STORY - by Helga

Each of us in the family went to confirmation classes at the Lutheran Church. Inger and I went through the classes together when she was fifteen, and I was thirteen. It was good to get the general Bible knowledge, but being "confirmed" did not always lead to a "change of heart" - that is, being convicted of our sinful, lost nature, and of the need to ask Jesus to save us.

For me, that change took place a year later when I was fourteen. It was in the fall of the same year that Laura and Paul came to faith in Christ - 1931. It came when we attended preaching services at the small mission chapel, a mile and a half walk from our home. Each night during the brisk October evenings, we would walk together with Aunt Sarah and Mom through the woods, our mother lighting the way with her lantern. Stars were twinkling, bright and clear on those cold nights. As I looked at the glorious display overhead, I would think of the greatness of God, the Creator of the heavens and the earth. *"When I consider Thy heavens, the work of Thy fingers, the moon and the stars, which Thou hast ordained; what is man that Thou art mindful of him? and the son of man, that Thou visitest him?"* (Psalm 8:4). I was overwhelmed at the thought that this great God loved me enough to send His son to make a way of salvation. *"For God so loved the world that He gave his only begotten Son, that whosoever believeth in Him should not perish but have everlasting life,"* (John 3:16). Yet, this preacher at the little Mission Chapel said, *"For all have sinned, and come short of the glory of God;"* (Romans 3:23). Although I loved the Lord at an early age because of Mom's and Grandma Kari's example, it was there in the little chapel in the woods that I was made aware of my sinful nature and of my need to humble myself before the Lord. There I publicly made it known that I was accepting the sacrifice Jesus made for my sins, and asking Him to rule in my heart.

The following spring I was baptized in a muddy river on someone's farm. I remember that my brother Karl was there. He stood on one side of me and the missionary on the other side to help as I was immersed.

My mother wrote me a note saying, "Dear Helga, Jesus said, *'I am the way, the truth, and the life: no man cometh unto the Father, but by me,'* (John 14:6). Don't forget to study your Bible, Helga. My prayers and my thoughts will go with you wherever you go. Love Mother"

*   *   *   *

## ELLEN'S STORY - by Ellen

In 1923 I started through confirmation classes. Since Reverend Fadum had four churches to care for, it was not strange that he could not meet with our confirmation classes any more often than he did. It was when the Ladies' Aid met once a month that he also would hold our classes. It took a long time for us to cover the doctrines of the church and the Bible history. It was almost three years from the time our class of fifteen first met until we were confirmed in June, 1926.

The last day we met with him before confirmation, Reverend Fadum had donned his gown and collar over his suit. Then he took each one of us separately into the small room behind the pulpit to personally speak with each of us concerning our relationship with God. When it came my turn, he told me that the Lord loved me and wanted me to be his child. All I had to do was ask Him to forgive me of my sins, and then thank Him for His great gift of salvation. I was sixteen, yet we had not been encouraged to express ourselves. In our home when other adults were around, children were taught to seldom be seen and never heard, so I couldn't open up to the Pastor. I suppose I just sat there and stared at him. Yet when I left the church, I could hardly wait until I got home to go upstairs and kneel in front of my father's old blue trunk. There I prayed the "Publican's prayer" in Norwegian as I had so often heard it in the Norwegian services, *"Gud, vær meg synder nådig!"* (God, be merciful to me, a needy sinner.) Now that prayer meant something to me. It meant that the burden of guilt and the fear of death were lifted and I was free. I had previously read John Bunyan's "Pilgrim's Progress," but had not understood it. Now I understood that it was the burden of guilt and sin that rolled off Christian's back when he came to the cross.

The change in me was great enough for the family to notice, even though I didn't tell anyone. Of course there were times when I still lost my temper, but I would feel badly about it afterward. I also continually prayed for myself and for others.

In the next five years, I struggled, wondering what I ought to do with my life. For several summers I went to Hibbing to get a job. We knew the Louis Carpenter family who lived there. Louis and his sister Delia, together with their dad, had homesteaded up north shortly after my parents settled on their land. Their father had wanted to come to the pioneer country, even though he was blind. By this time, the father had passed away, and Louis with his wife and children had moved to Hibbing. They always made me welcome to stay with them whenever I came looking for work. In those days, anyone who was anyone, kept a maid, so it wasn't hard to find a job, and I did fine with cleaning duties.

One summer I worked a full three months as a waitress. It was different and interesting, but I was timid to work with the public. I tried to overcome my shyness, but the customers loved to tease me, knowing they could easily make me blush. Then, too, my feet were often hurting. I nearly crippled them, especially the day I wore new patent leather shoes! Although I made better wages than I had as a maid, I tired of the job that had me on my feet so much.

One spring, Ma's old friend, Emma, came up to Nass. She and a couple who ran the section house in Saginaw came to spend a weekend. I got up early to make waffles for them. Mr. J. was quite impressed by this husky-looking young girl who liked to get up and make breakfast. Other girls they had hired at the section house wouldn't get up to cook breakfast for the crew. Not long after that, I received a letter from them, asking me to come to Saginaw and help them out. They promised better wages than I had ever received, so I went to Saginaw for the summer. I knew there would be a lot of work with six or seven men and a family with five kids to cook for. I didn't know how much extra I would be doing, like the family washing, some ironing and cleaning. I had naturally assumed that I would be Mrs. J's assistant, but she sat and held the baby all day, and seldom put her down in her crib, even when she was sleeping. She was relieved that I could converse with her in Swedish, but she actually didn't talk much – just sat and sighed, "Oh I wish I was back in Sweden! We had so much fun there."

The first morning I went into the pantry and reached up for a package of cereal. A mouse jumped down on my hand and ran up to my shoulder. I jumped, but I didn't scream. I shuddered for a second before daring to proceed with my next move. I had decided against putting that cereal on the table, so I tried other packages. Mice hopped out of other cereal or cracker packages. At last I found an unopened one and set that on the table. When I told Mr. J. about it, he merely shrugged his shoulders and laughed. I set traps and tried my best to get rid of them, but they still ran all over the house, especially the pantry.

I cooked on a wood range, and there were some very hot days in July and August. There wasn't a cook book in the place, and I wasn't a very experienced cook. I did make a fairly edible meal of meat, potatoes, and vegetables, but I made some disastrous pies. Mr. J. informed me that they liked waffles, biscuits or pancakes quite often for supper. It was very time consuming to make those. I had to begin in the middle of the afternoon. It took time to heat the waffle iron on that stove. I would make enough for the family, and then I'd make another stack before the men came in for supper at five o'clock.

I don't know why I stayed there all summer. Perhaps it was because no one really supervised my work, and it was indeed a "steady" job. It certainly was not because of any of the men. The ones who stayed in the bunk house were middle-aged Swedish bachelors. Only one was closer to my age. He was very happy to find a young lady who could converse in his language, but the prospect didn't interest me. He was a braggart as well as a heavy drinker.

There was too much work in the heat of the summer, but strangely enough it wasn't until four of the family's children went off to school each day that I began to get restless. I had no place to go on my time off except to stay in my room and read or to take long walks on Sunday afternoons. As the fall deepened and the leaves began to fall, I knew I couldn't stay there much longer. One cold Sunday afternoon, after a long walk by the lake, I came back and announced that I would be leaving in a week, if they wanted to look for another girl.

Mr. J. looked disappointed, "We had hoped you would stay through the winter and be with us next summer." I just shook my head and went wearily up to my room.

If ever I was trying to "find myself" it was that summer of 1931. I was twenty-one, and I was just drifting between staying home and working out for a few months at a time. Laura was married and settled down. Perhaps that, among other things, set me to thinking. *Where will I be five years from now?* I knew I didn't want to be somebody's maid or hired girl for the rest of my life. After I had been home a few weeks, I told Ma that

I didn't know what I wanted out of life. To earn money for clothes didn't interest me – probably because I wasn't exactly a fashion model!

Ma looked at me with a loving, understanding expression. "Perhaps you would like to be a missionary?" she suggested.

I pondered the thought and nodded, "Yes, perhaps I would."

Ma must have talked with the young ladies who were serving in the Northern Gospel Mission's station west of us, because it wasn't long before they came to call on me, and give me information about their alma maters. One was a Moody Bible Institute graduate, the other was from Northwestern Bible School in Minneapolis. I looked over the information, but when I learned the cost of tuition, it was far beyond what I could make, even if I worked several years. Then Mr. Welliver, the head of the Northern Gospel Mission, sent me literature about a smaller Bible college in Kansas City, Missouri, in which he was an instructor. It also listed names of graduates, many of whom had worked in our community. My younger brothers and sisters had attended their Vacation Bible Schools, and were always singing the catchy little choruses they learned. I had secretly longed to attend too, but I was much older than the other kids.

As I stayed home the remainder of that winter, I thanked God that He was giving my life new meaning and direction.
*"Trust in the Lord with all thine heart; and lean not unto thine own understanding. In all thy ways acknowledge Him, and He shall direct thy paths." (Prov. 3:5,6)*

## Chapter 22
## PREPARING TO SERVE
### by Ellen

Early in the summer of 1932, I went to Hibbing for one more job to earn more money for Bible college. I found a very pleasant, quiet place to work with an elderly doctor and his wife. I became their home answering service, and live-in maid. His wife also wanted to discuss her associated charities with me, different ways to serve through the Salvation Army. I attended their services with them. For the most part the services were separate from their charity work, although some members were people who had been helped. The friendly captain and his wife wanted me to go to their training school and become an officer in the "army." Although my friend, Mrs. C. wore the Salvation Army bonnet and sold their magazine *The War Cry*, it did not seem the right thing for me to do.

While out walking one evening, I heard a voice shouting, and spotted a big tent pitched at the far end of the block. The closer I came, the louder and more frenzied the shouting. With curiosity I slipped inside and took a seat near the opening. A young man on the platform was working himself into a sweat. At one point he loosened his tie, and slipped it off. After that, he unbuttoned his shirt. When he tossed that aside, I wondered what was coming next! There were a lot of "Glory hallelujahs," and "Praise the Lord," coming from the swaying audience, but I had seen quite enough. When I got up to leave, I found the opening blocked by a few of his followers. They didn't want me to leave, but when I insisted that I knew the Lord, and had also received the Holy Ghost at the time I was saved, they let me go.

It was indeed a summer in which I was searching for the right expression of my faith in the Lord. I discovered that there were many ways of serving - as many ways as there are different personalities and callings.

I had sent my application to the Gospel Missionary Union in Kansas City, and had been accepted, so, although I didn't know how God would be using me, I trusted that he would make the way clear. The Gospel Missionary Union had been established a generation or so earlier to train missionaries for the foreign fields. Then as immigrants, particularly from the Scandinavian and Slavic countries were homesteading in northern Minnesota, the training school supplied workers to the stations up north to help reach these pioneers. Anyone who hoped to go to a foreign mission field, first had to have a period of in-training service with the Northern Gospel Mission in northern Minnesota.

I arrived by bus in Kansas City, Missouri, on New Year's Eve, 1932. In northern Minnesota I was used to having snow on the ground from November to April, so I felt like a misplaced Eskimo in my fake fur coat, my suede beret, and fur-topped boots over my shoes. There wasn't a speck of snow, and the weather was warm and spring-like that afternoon in Kansas City. As I rang the doorbell and stood waiting in front of the three-story brick building, I looked about me. The location wasn't the most attractive. That area of the city near Independence Avenue had degenerated into low-rent apartment buildings – structures that had formerly been mansions of the wealthy. Those were the years of Depression, bootlegging moonshine, and gangsters. We had always heard that the Chicago gangsters went down to Kansas City to live, so I was not too surprised when I heard a lot of shooting during the night. I wasn't frightened though because I felt certain they wouldn't dare enter the building with the big sign, "Gospel Missionary Union," over the front door.

The following morning as I waited in the hall for the second bell, signaling breakfast, I looked at the other students, most of whom I had met the evening before. I expected someone to mention the shooting I had heard, but no one said anything. Once seated at the table, the long prayer over, and the eating and conversation going on, I finally found a chance to ask those at my table if they heard the shooting. They looked blank at first, and then one of the young men said, "Oh, you mean the car that was back-firing in the alley? It was just one of the colored boys bringing in the New Year." ("Colored" was the polite, accepted term for black people back then.)

From the jobs I had had in Saginaw, and in Hibbing, I managed to save enough money to cover the cost of part of my room and board for a few weeks. I worked a few hours a day to make up the rest. We had a very tight schedule, so I was grateful that at first I had the extra time I needed for study. Eventually I had to work for all of my room and board, as most of the students were doing, so we all struggled to find sufficient study time.

I was on kitchen detail, making breakfast with the help of another girl, but there wasn't much to cook. There was seldom enough money in the housekeeping fund for groceries.

Sometimes the man who ran the printing press would bring in some milk from his little farm. When he did, we would cook a huge kettleful of cornmeal or cracked wheat. Since we were always hungry, it was very tasty. Sometimes we ate it without milk. Once or twice a week, one of the men would drive in his jalopy to a bakery in the city and would bring back huge canvas bags full of three, or four-day-old bread. We were grateful for anything. Meat, vegetables, and fruits were scarce at times. Sometimes on a Saturday the little Italian grocery across the street had specials on hamburger. At ten or twelve cents a pound, Mr. Hawks could buy enough for a meal of meat loaf or meat balls – but we were never to have it for a Sunday dinner! He wanted nothing cooking in the kitchen that would distract anyone from Sunday morning services.

One Sunday I discovered how he felt, when I was the one in charge of preparing dinner and had a roast in the oven. I knew it was a sacred trust that I could not betray by letting the roast burn. As I sat, trying to keep my attention on Mr. Hawks' sermon, I could just smell that roast burning. Every nerve in my body was alert. Finally, I could no longer sit still. I was in the front row since I had played for the opening songs, but I didn't think I would cause too much disturbance if I would slip out and go down the hall to the kitchen.

When I returned, Mr. Hawks was making a long pause. He often did that, so I paid no attention, but the grins and giggles as I sat down among the girls, caused me to wonder. As soon as we had sung the last song, and he had pronounced the final "amen," the girls followed me back to the kitchen laughing and complimenting me on how calmly I took it. When I asked what they were talking about, one of them said, "Didn't you notice that he wasn't speaking when you came back? He never said a word after you walked out – just stood there, staring out the window and waiting!" So, directly or indirectly, the Sunday roast and I were the cause of some very simple dinners from then on! Mr. Hawks, who was from a strict Puritan New England background, said, "An apple and a piece of bread should be enough for anyone's Sunday dinner." Luckily for us, the housekeeper would not agree to that. To begin with, we did not have a regular breakfast on Sunday mornings. Everyone took an apple and a slice or two of bread up to his or her room on Saturday night. Sunday morning was to be spent in Bible reading, prayer and meditation. Admittedly, most of the students just slept longer.

Beans and bread pudding were two of the mainstays, especially on wash day when there were no classes, and everyone was assigned a task. Since my digestive problem was again going in full force, I could not eat those two staples. I would retire to the pantry with a cup of hot water, and a piece of bread, most of the time without butter. I had very little to eat some days, but after a few weeks I wasn't even hungry. I was so engrossed in Bible study that I literally lived on the Word of God. Yet, after I had lost twenty pounds in the first two months, I began to feel listless and weak.

By the time I went home in May, I had lost forty pounds, in five months! That was the fastest weight loss I ever made! I had to drink half and half cream to regain my strength. Then I went to work for a lawyer's family who were staying in their summer home. I was not overworked, I had nourishing food, and each day I had a relaxing time at the lake with four of their five children. As for my Bible training, the first three months that I had missed before entering at New Years in 1933, I made up by correspondence during the summer months.

The folks were still living at Nass, but were preparing to move to Chisholm. In the past five years the store had steadily lost business. It was chiefly due to the coming of the automobile. As more and more families got their own car, they found they could get their groceries and other supplies cheaper if they drove to Cook.

Then, too, with the Depression, fewer families in the region were asking for Pa's services with his portable saw rig. Some who did ask for some work to be done would settle their debt by giving Pa an old car, or a piece of land. In this way we obtained a lake property on Black Duck Lake north of Gheen. There was no road around to this piece of land, so Dad would park the car and cross the lake by boat. For this, Dad built a big, flat bottom boat so it would be easier to haul a lot of tools and equipment for building a cabin and getting it ready for use. Pa was also given a small property one mile north of Chisholm. It was to that rock covered hill that they moved in the summer of '33.

Pa had moved the saw rig to the place near Chisholm and set it up permanently, thinking there would be more lumber jobs near town, but the Depression was still keeping progress down.

The "boys" then got jobs working for a man who ran a logging company. Johnny, Karl and even Ingvald, age 13, worked in McKusick's garage to keep a fleet of trucks in running order. Johnny was a fairly good mechanic, but Karl was the real expert. Ingvald proved to have the same talent for motors that Karl did. He was far too young to be working steadily, and should have spent five days a week in school, but he played truant as often as he dared, so he could help at the garage. They worked long hours and even were called out at night – especially Karl who was a top mechanic. One night he went to sleep at the wheel and woke up to find himself skirting a deep ditch. Perhaps that near accident was what caused him to turn to the Lord. Not long after that he made the decision to go to Bible college in the fall. He knew his two brothers could carry on the work.

That September I didn't have to worry about how to get to Kansas City, since my brother had a car. Karl had never been a bookworm, and never enjoyed school, so I had my reservations about how he would do as a student. We had been there only a week or so when he began to get homesick. The staff had let us use a visitor's room where I could help my brother with his study hour. His mind would wander away from the Bible Doctrine, Church History, English, or whatever subject we were trying to study – or I was trying to study. Instead he would talk about the boys, wondering what they would be doing in the garage. Then when he became a good pal of Scotty, there was not much use in trying to direct his mind into practical channels. Scotty was a very untutored boy from Leavenworth, who thought he would try being a Bible college student while on a few months' leave from guard duty. The two of them could only talk and dream about the day when they would be great preachers – of which there wasn't much likelihood.

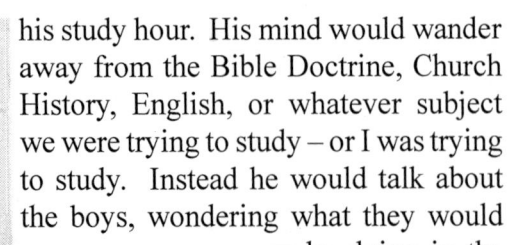

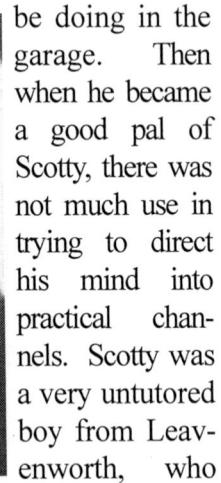

PHOTO: Karl and Ellen 1934

Scotty returned to guard duty after his leave was up, but Karl never did become a good student. He didn't need to. He already had his calling, for his true talent could not be hidden. Mr. Jones, the president of the school and mission board, was having trouble with his car. Karl fixed it. The furnace quit working. Karl fixed it. The linotype machine broke down. Karl fixed it. Then Joe, the linotype operator, showed Karl how to work it, and soon Karl was taking his turn at the linotype. He and Joe became good friends.

Karl fixed watches for all the men – a skill he probably learned from his father. He did not charge for the work, but only for the parts that he bought at a jeweler's downtown. He visited the jeweler so often that the man asked him if he would stay and work for him during the summer. However, when spring came,

Karl could think of nothing but getting home again, back to his beloved North Country, and back to his trade as a full-time mechanic. He did not return to school with me in the fall. I graduated in May 1935, having completed a three-year course.

## Chapter 23
## AWAY FROM THE HOMESTEAD
by Helga

PHOTO 1933: Gilbertson Siblings.
Back row: Paul Rostvit, Johnny, Inger, a friend, Karl, Ellen.
Front row: Laura, Ingvald, Agnes, and Helga.

Grandmother Kari was terminally ill in 1933 and was in the hospital in Hibbing. After she died, Uncle Harry and his wife moved back to Florida, and Uncle Joe moved to a place near the homestead. That same summer we also left the homestead to move to Chisholm. One of our cousins, Albert, with his wife Edith moved to our homestead to keep the post office open.

Our home near Chisholm had white siding with blue trim, so it may have looked better than the tarpaper covered building on the homestead, but we would learn that in the winter it would be a cold home just the same. There were no storm windows, nor storm doors, and since there was no basement the floors were very cold. Being newly built, it was not finished under the eaves, so cold winds, or even snow blew in at times. All winter, we would huddle around the stove and freeze.

When we moved to Chisholm, I was sixteen. To my surprise, in early summer, Edward Rostvit came to see me. Having borrowed Paul's Model A, he took me for a short ride. He had always loved driving and was a good driver. He told me of his trip from their homestead, west of Bear River. He had had two blowouts on the way, at which times the tire had to be taken off, a patch put on the inner tube, put it back on and pump it up again.

He came to see me several times that summer. Each trip averaged about 15 miles between flat tires. We enjoyed each other's company. Edward had a great sense of humor so he often had me laughing as he related some adventure he had been through. He turned more serious, though, as he related the plans he had for the coming months. Having finished the ten grades available at Togo School, he planned to board in Grand Rapids, some fifty miles from his homestead, to complete his final two years of high school there. I was sad to think I wouldn't be seeing him as often.

* * * *

From the time that my dad brought the first Model T to the Nass area in 1916, he was never without a car. Through the years, he traded for newer models and makes periodically. I remember a Model T touring car with two black leather seats. It had a top and side curtains that snapped closed for protection in rainy weather. There was a Model A with the hard top and there was a succession of other cars, such as: Chevrolet, Buick, Star,

PHOTO: Karl's Austin

Dort, and an Essex that really belonged to Johnny. At one time, Karl had an Austin – smaller than the Volkswagons of today. The small car was so rare that everyone noticed it. More than once while stopped at a stop light, some young men would come and lift it off the ground. Karl got tired of that nonsense so he wired it. When others laid their hands on it, Karl turned on a switch. They would get a shock and let go fast.

That fall, Ellen and Karl were in Bible college in Kansas City, (1933-34). I missed them. I saw Ellen very seldom since between college years she would get jobs, but I rejoiced that she was enjoying her studies. Karl was a quiet and kind-hearted brother. He turned out to be a blessing to the small college as a general handyman. After the one year in Kansas City, he returned, enjoying getting back with his brother Johnny doing mechanic work.

That first fall in Chisholm, I returned to school. Because I had stayed out of school for two years, Agnes and I now would be together in the ninth grade. I enjoyed school and dreamed of graduating with Agnes, but she decided to quit. At that time it was common for many to have only eight years of schooling. My youngest brother Ingvald was in the seventh grade.

For me, going to school in town was different. Where there had been nine of us in the eighth grade in Togo, there were nearly 300 ninth graders and a total of 850 students in the big three-story school building in Chisholm – one floor per grade. There were only three minutes between classes. The halls were so packed with students going different directions that it was chaos! Sometimes I was momentarily swept along with the crowd in the opposite direction from the classroom I was heading for. In time, I got used to pushing my way through the crowd. If I stayed timid, I'd be tardy for my next class.

Chisholm was known for having an excellent education system. I took history, English, algebra and home economics - half the year was cooking, the other half, sewing. We were also required to take gymnasium twice a week and swimming class once a week. Since many people drown in Minnesota's 10,000 lakes each year, a law was passed that all larger schools had to have swimming pools and it was mandatory for all students to learn to swim. I did well in most of the classes, but admittedly I disliked studying history!

Cooking classes were fun and there was no homework involved. We could eat the things we cooked and that was a treat when we had so little at home. Even though a 1 ½ pound loaf of bread was only 9 cents, and a pound of hamburger was only a nickel, we did not always have the nickel! If we did get some hamburger to go with the potatoes and rutabagas from our garden, we had a pretty good meal, but that menu was repeated and repeated, all winter! We had cornmeal mush or else pancakes for breakfast all winter too. No wonder we enjoyed the things we cooked at school! After six weeks, we got our first report card. I made it on the A Honor Roll. One month, my history grade was down so I slipped to the B Honor Roll. After that, I tried harder to get the grades back up.

Most students walked home for lunch, but we bus students could not. Most often, I brought my own sandwich and ate the bowl of free soup given to us each day. We bought lunch tickets for 25 cents and we spent it as we chose. We could get a sandwich – two pieces of bread with only butter between for one cent; a glass of milk for one cent; or dessert for two cents – usually pudding made by students in the cooking classes.

The following summer I worked at a strawberry farm at Orr. I lived with the older couple who ran the farm. My work was cooking, cleaning, and washing dishes. I worked seven days a week with time off to go to church with the couple on Sundays. The church was run by the Northern Gospel Mission. I was seventeen and got homesick through the long summer, but I stuck with it and earned thirty dollars for school clothes. I bought several new dresses and a skirt and blouse.

In my sophomore year, I entered the senior high school. I enjoyed geometry, even to the memorization of all those theorems. Another subject was biology, but that teacher was something else! She was built tall and angular, her hair was never fixed neatly, and she wore sloppy brown dresses. When she lectured, she stood behind her desk, gripping the edge of the desk – palms toward the class, and her arms bent the wrong way. She must have been double-jointed, but it made her look like an over-sized grasshopper. (Oops! That wasn't nice, but she made us dissect frogs and grasshoppers, and she crammed evolution down our throats until I thought, *(if she can believe that ridiculous evolution idea, maybe she herself evolved from a grasshopper!)*

    I was notified by the Dean of Girls, that I was a member of an exclusive society of girls with a high grade average. It didn't interest me at all. The other girls were daughters of prominent business people in Chisholm who had money. They dressed in fine silk dresses or nice pastel-colored wool skirts and sweaters. I was poor and a shy country girl, so I felt out of place in their company and really had nothing in common with them, except my grades.

    When Ingvald finished eighth grade, he enjoyed working full-time at the garage with his brothers. Inger lived in the apartment over the garage to keep house and to cook for "the boys." At that point, Dad was out of work, so Ingvald contributed fifteen dollars a month to help with expenses. We grew a lot of vegetables and potatoes and together with the fifteen dollars, we four who were still at home, Mom, Dad, Agnes and I, ate three meals a day. If Ingvald had not so cheerfully and willingly done that, I never could have graduated from high school. I will always be grateful to him for that.

    We were still in the midst of the Depression and times were tough. There wasn't a dime to spare for anything. I couldn't even go to a school play because it cost ten cents. Months later Dad got employment as a night watchman for the garage run by the township in nearby Balkan. The job didn't pay much, but he relished his responsibility of protecting the township's property from thieves.

*    *    *    *

    Edward Rostvit graduated in 1935 from his high school in Grand Rapids. I was elated when Ingvald offered to drive me there to see his graduation. Although I was glad to see the ceremony, I faced some disappointment in having very little time to see Edward. He was busy afterward with plans that his family and friends had for him. My one consolation was that in the short time I had for congratulating him, he slipped me one of his senior pictures.

That summer, Edward left Minnesota to work in the harvest fields of North Dakota. There he could earn $5.00 a day instead of the usual $1.00 a day he would get in timber work. I knew he didn't have a car that he could depend on to go that far. He would hitchhike or hop on freight trains to get there. I often looked at the photo of his handsome face, and would pray that God would protect and guide him. Although I didn't know where Edward was, God knew. Later I learned that after the harvest, Edward caught the freights to go to Montana where work was available for building a dam at Fort Peck. From there he went on to the West Coast.

* * * *

Meanwhile, that same year, May 1935, Ellen had persevered and completed the three years of studies in the Bible college, graduating as their star student. She was immediately placed to work at various mission stations back up in northern Minnesota.

## Chapter 24
## MISSION WORK UP NORTH
### By Ellen

Following my graduation, we all spent a week at a Bible and Missionary Conference in Mildred, Minnesota. Also, many workers who had been serving in the various mission stations up north were there, having a refreshing and inspiring break. Mr. and Mrs. Welliver, founders of the Northern Gospel Mission, had once owned a farm near Mildred, and the conference was held in the front yard of that farm. A huge tent was set up where the meetings were held. Cooking was done in the farm kitchen, but the meals were served outside, so we ate picnic style. I don't know what provisions would be made for rainy weather, but neither can I recall any.

After the conference, I was teamed with Anna, a jolly little girl with twinkling eyes, who was from a Mennonite background. We drove back up north in the little old coupe she used and settled down in the Sturgeon River community where we were to substitute for George and Olga Weiss. We had seen them at the conference, but they were remaining in the Mildred area to visit for a couple of weeks. A chapel had not been built yet in the Sturgeon River community. The Weisses lived in a small, one-room shack while serving three outlying communities. We had to use every penny we had to "feed the car," as Anna put it. Gasoline was probably about 35 cents a gallon then. We were in what was termed a "faith work," and as one of the girls said, "We trust in the Lord, and our parents and churches support us." I had no church support and my parents had barely enough to get along at home.

We found only some dark flour in the cabin. Anna made some very coarse bread with it. There were big, delicious Juneberries in the bushes around the cabin, but the combination of the berries and the dark bread did disastrous things to our digestive systems. Finally we did manage to get 25 pounds of flour and a kind farmer gave us some potatoes.

One night we heard someone bumping against the outside wall. I lay as still as I could, trying not to wake Anna, but finally I realized that she, too, was awake. We heard some shuffling, grunting noises, and then all was quiet again. I don't think either of us could go back to sleep. In the morning we found some tracks in the sand around the shack. Anna said, "It must have been that man in the community who is considered to be a peculiar character, but why would he take his little boy out at night – and they were both barefooted!" I began to laugh as soon as I saw the human-like footprints. A mother bear and her cub had been circling the shack, no doubt in search of food.

I substituted in several areas that summer. In each mission station I moved to, I had different working partners - some were more of a delight than others. By fall I was in Rainier, right on the Canadian border. I recall the sight of the enormously bright beam of light sweeping across the Rainy River from the Canadian side and thinking, oh that I might be as that bright light in a dark world. Philippians 2:14, *"Do all things without murmurings and disputings: that ye may be blameless and harmless, the sons of God, without rebuke, in the midst of a crooked and perverse nation, among whom ye shine as lights in the world."*

In October I received orders to go down to Gheen, which was to be my winter station. I had orders, but no money to get there! However, the girl working with me loaned me two dollars for my train ticket. When I arrived at the Gheen station I discovered I was to have the honor of living in the largest station on the circuit. There was a big chapel. The living room and kitchen were situated in the back part of the building. There was a little cook stove in the kitchen, a heater in the living room and a huge jacketed school-house type stove in the chapel. Upstairs over the chapel was a storage and sleeping area. When I arrived that fall morning I was surprised to see four girls there. One was the worker who regularly served in Rainier. She was on her way back there after her vacation. Two others were headed to Orr, just a few miles up the line from Gheen. The fourth one was Merle Bunker, the regular worker at Gheen. She had been there for some time, but was a candidate for South America, so she hoped to be sent out soon. She was to remain at the station until she had trained me as a replacement.

Merle was a husky-built, square sort of a girl with a cast-iron constitution. She was cooking corn meal mush when I came. Everyone received a generous portion of it, but I asked her not to dish up any for me. There was bread and jam on the table. She said, jokingly, "I hope you're not one of those finicky eaters because we won't be having any dainty meals." Then the other three began discussing psychosomatic illnesses while I ate my bread and jam and drank my hot water in silence. I knew they considered me a stupid backwoods person because I was one of the natives of this region in which they were doing missionary work. I simply let them continue to think so. It takes so little to make some people happy! Yet I had a great advantage over the workers from other states. It didn't take me long to get to know the families of the town and the surrounding farming area because I was one of them. I had grown up just about fifteen miles across the woods – as the crow flies – probably more like twenty miles along the winding roads. Also, for befriending others who were Scandinavians, I had the advantage of speaking Norwegian or Swedish.

Merle gave me a brief summary on some of the problems I might run into. There was an atheists' club to which most of the men of the area belonged. They had taken an oath never to believe in God, yet they did permit their wives and children to attend services and Sunday School at the chapel. I thought it was the saddest blasphemy I had ever heard of.

There was one elderly Norwegian lady who was married to a Swedish man of the atheists' group. She had been having the missionary ladies come to her house one afternoon each week for Bible reading and discussion. She understood the American language quite adequately, but she would read from her Norwegian Bible. When I began to converse with her in Norwegian, she was delighted. We would never see the husband. Whenever Merle and I were at her house, he would be working or just staying outside. He would bring her to our church services but would not stay for fear the other men would know he had been in the Lord's house.

After Merle left for Kansas City to make preparations to go to South America, I was on my own for a few weeks. I had the use of the old Chevrolet to get out to the places I visited during the week. Later, I finally met the Norwegian lady's husband. I caught a glimpse of him in the doorway as his wife and I were having an interesting discussion. When we had closed our Bibles, he walked into the kitchen and made some teasing remark in Swedish and I gave him a proper rejoinder. He grinned and came closer. He sat at the table with us for afternoon lunch and learned about my background.

The very next Sunday when he brought his wife to morning services, he stayed, mumbling something like, "I may just as well stay as to drive back and forth again." He sat in a back row and pretended he was just waiting for his wife. Once, as I was speaking, I chanced to glance in his direction. He had such a sad, longing look in his eyes! Of course, when he caught me looking directly at him, he turned and stared out the window as if he had no interest at all. Many years later when one of the workers wrote and told me that the man had died, and that he had confessed that he had believed and trusted in the Lord for a long time, I kind of liked to believe I might have had a little something to do with it.

The only time I was nervous about staying alone was when the lumberjacks from a nearby logging camp were on strike. I could plainly hear them shouting and fighting, making a general racket around the tavern which was only a block away from the chapel. Before going to bed at night, I would take a flashlight and search the chapel thoroughly. We didn't keep a fire going in the big chapel stove so I would even check inside the jacket of the stove.

As long as Merle was with me, I had food. She seemed to have some regular support because she was never out of money. When she left, there was still quite a bit of food left in the pantry. Before another worker came, however, I was nearly all out of food. When Velma came late in the fall, I soon discovered that she was just as poor as I was. We were poorer than a couple of chapel mice. We couldn't even get any nourishment from the glue that fastened the pages of the song books together, as the mice did if they were permitted to live long enough.

On one occasion I thought I should show my faith by starting to mix a batch of bread dough before going to the post office. We had no flour, so I started it with cornmeal, trusting that some money would come in and I could buy flour on my way home. Merle, being the native Iowan that she was, had left us a lot of corn meal. The post office stop was fruitless, and that yeast bread, made of pure yellow corn meal, was the coarsest bread I ever ate.

Sometimes it helped to pray specifically for exactly the item that we needed, *"Ask and ye shall receive..."* (Mt. 6:7). After eating jam and bread for a long time, I craved butter. One morning I specifically asked the Lord to send us some butter. A little later when I walked down to the post office to get the mail, the postmistress handed me a big bowlful of butter. She said, "You know, it was the strangest thing. As I sat down to eat breakfast this morning, I suddenly thought that you girls might need some butter."

I thanked her and told her how very welcome it was because we were all out of butter. I couldn't tell her there had been no butter at the chapel for several weeks – ever since I arrived in Gheen. Nor could I tell her that there was seldom much of any kind of food. As had also happened in other stations where I had worked, our food offerings ran in streaks. If we were given a quart of milk at the beginning of the week, we would receive two or three more from other sources that week. If the week began with a meat offering, we would get more of the same that week. Yet, those weeks of plenty did not happen very often in Gheen.

That winter of 1935-36 was one of the coldest on record. The walls snapped and crackled at night. One night there was an unusually sharp report. Velma sat up and whispered, "What was that?"

I thought I was exaggerating wildly when I answered jokingly, "Oh, it always snaps like that when it gets down to 50 below zero." To my surprise when I went out the next morning to look at our neighbor's thermometer, it was slightly colder than 50 below. When I told Velma, she thought I was still kidding, so she had to check for herself. That afternoon we did not hike the two miles out in the country to have a little Bible class with the dear old Norwegian lady.

Perhaps that was the morning Velma had a problem with her teeth freezing. We had been sleeping on a pullout couch in the living room during the winter, as it would have been impossible to sleep in the unheated upstairs. Even the living room got too cold some of those extremely frigid nights. That morning it was Velma's turn to get the fire going and make breakfast. When I came into the kitchen, she was fumbling over the stove. I made a remark, but she just mumbled some reply. As I stepped up to the stove to warm my hands, I could see the reason for her silence. She would never look in my direction or attempt to talk until she had her dentures in her mouth, and they were frozen solid in the cup of water that she was trying to thaw out. She was about 27 years old, and already had dentures! [She later went to Columbia, South America, and worked there until retirement age, after which she worked at one of the new mission stations in Mexico.]

I had gone to Bible college because I wanted to go to a foreign field – preferably Morocco. But Mr. Welliver said that because of my poor health, and the fact that I had no financial backing, he would never recommend me for a foreign field. He knew of my allergy to eggs, and he, having been a missionary in Morocco, admitted that sometimes they chiefly lived on eggs. For me, even in my home region of northern Minnesota, my digestive problems, which grew worse and worse, were a matter of constant caution on my part. We were nearly always treated to coffee, cake, rolls or cookies – four items that were like poison to me. At one home I ate a cinnamon roll because she set only coffee and rolls on the table for us. I was in constant pain every step of the way home. The dear Norwegian lady set out an assortment of breads, cheese, and meat. She also had the lightest, most delicious looking cinnamon rolls, and she told me there was only one egg in the entire batch, but I didn't dare take the chance.

Of course, I needed a more balanced diet that would include more fruits and vegetables. We did get some once in a while, like when a farmer gave us a lot of green tomatoes. It was as Mr. Hawks told us at the Bible college, "In this kind of work you must be prepared to be full and to suffer want – which translated means that you have the turkey one week and the feathers the next week." Well, we never did have turkey.

We did enjoy at least one good chicken dinner at the home of the section boss. He had gone back to Greece and brought home a beautiful young wife. They had two little daughters, and when we came on the scene she could speak and understand enough to enjoy having company. We just dropped in for an afternoon call, and she insisted on preparing a fried chicken supper for us. She fried it in olive oil, and it was the most delicious and digestible meal I ever ate! She was also a bright conversationalist, full of humor and laughter. We enjoyed her very much. There was also a Polish bachelor who raised a field of cabbage, from which he occasionally brought us a head. One time after dark, he smuggled some venison to us. We didn't know quite how such an illegal gift should be received, but decided to accept, be thankful, and enjoy it.

Gheen was about a mile off the main highway. Karl drove past many times, but he said it was usually late at night when he was on one of his emergency calls. Then late one evening, he stopped in with a big box full of groceries. It contained several grapefruit, a few pounds of wieners, besides macaroni, rice and other staples. Although we could have enjoyed the whole treasure, both Velma and I were thinking of the family at the Orr station a few miles up the highway who had two hungry teenage boys. It just happened that they called on us that week, so we gave them the biggest portion of our food gift. It was a joy to share it with those who were more needy than ourselves. *"It is more blessed to give than to receive,"* (Acts 20:35b).

This was a tough life for families, or for singles, especially ones like myself who had little or no financial backing. I did not want to remain an old maid missionary in the Northern Gospel Mission for the rest of my life. I had seen too many examples of what that kind of life would be like.

PHOTO: Through relatives of my stepfather, I met Edward Gilbertson and his sister, Mattie.

Then there was also the matter of a tall, slim, pleasant, blue-eyed farmer in North Dakota. We had been carrying on a correspondence that I initiated six years earlier. It had started after Pa and Ma took Grandma Kari and her new husband, Erik, to Cooperstown, North Dakota, to visit with Grandma's sister, Gunhild. When they came back, Ma told me about Gunhild's youngest son, Edward Gilbertson, who lived alone in a large farm house. [He was a first cousin to my stepfather, but no relation to me since my father had been Hans Skoglie.]

Ma said, "Edward is very shy, and very nice." Then she suggested, "Why don't you write to him?" I wrote. He answered, and the correspondence continued in an "off-and-on" way while I was out working, when I went to Bible college, and when I was serving up north in the mission stations. Perhaps I had written only one or two brief letters a year.

In the fall of 1935 while at Gheen, I received a letter from him in which he told me that he and his brother, John, were planning to pay the family a short visit before proceeding down to Minneapolis to visit their sister, Gunhild.

Velma and I drove to Chisholm in the forenoon, so we were at the folks' place when John and Edward arrived late in the afternoon. I remember thinking that Edward was very red-faced and sunburned, but most of the redness was probably caused by blushing! We didn't talk much that first evening. There were too many pairs of eyes watching and trying to make predictions. Ma's and Pa's eyes were on us constantly, and Velma was barely keeping the smirks and giggles under control. I escaped to do the dishes as soon as I could after supper. Velma returned to Gheen the next morning. One of my brothers would drive me back when the time came.

PHOTO:
Edward and Ellen

The following day after dinner, Pa, thinking he was being very diplomatic, arose from the table and said to Edward's brother, "We'd better go outside and look around, and leave these two alone." Then to cap it off, he said to us, "You two, who have corresponded for so long, should have a lot to talk about." I again retreated to the kitchen to wash the dishes, then Edward picked up the dish towel to help me. When there were no longer the prying eyes and ears nearby, we were able to talk, just 'get-to-know-you' talk. Later that afternoon as we walked the old road to Chisholm, we talked some more. We visited the boys at the garage, and Inger upstairs in the apartment where she cooked for them. Edward and John only stayed a couple of days, so we didn't have many opportunities to talk, but the letter exchange was more frequent after that.

I finished the winter in the mission work. By springtime I was invited to North Dakota. Many of Edward's relatives, no doubt, were curious to meet me. I was well escorted as Karl drove his car, Ingvald furnished the gas, and Inger and Johnny came for the ride to see the place they hoped would be my future home.

\* \* \* \*

It was a cold day, June 2, 1936, when Edward and I were married by the pastor of his church. It was the summer of the big

PHOTO: Edward and Ellen Gilbertson's North Dakota home.

drought for North Dakota. The entire nation, or at least down through the middle and into the southwestern states, had been in the dust bowl years. I believe 1936 was the last of a series of very dry years, at least it proved to be so for North Dakota. It was hot that summer. One day it reached 117 degrees! We survived by spending the day in the basement. I had dreamed of having flowers all over the place as Mom had in her yard. I bought flower seeds and dug up little flower beds all over the yard, but the only thing that grew was Russian thistles that broke loose in the wind and went rolling across the yard and over the fields. It was the major crop in the fields, too. Some farmers cut the tumble weeds while they were green and stacked them for hay. The harvest that year was sad. The men came with the threshing rig and worked for half a day to get the few kernels of wheat, rye, and oats. Here and there through the fields, where the low spots maintained a little moisture, a few stalks had grown and headed out with miniature kernels. The crew had started after dinner and was finished by coffee time. They stood around with their heads down in despair.

Things began to look up the next year, though, and from then on it was up all the way. Some years were not so good, but they averaged out to good maintenance crops at least. I was a farmer's wife, and I thanked the Lord that Edward was a God-fearing man who relied on Him.

## Chapter 25
## TRIUMPHS AND TRAGEDY
### By Helga

While I was busy in high school studies, my brother Johnny was away from home, working. He was driving trucks, hauling timber from up north and into town. As he passed through the regions where many homesteads had been, he stopped at the Sturgeon River Chapel to visit with the George Weiss family. He had a hunch that the young couple with an infant son were probably out of food. Those small mission stations had little or no support for those dedicated young folks in that depression time. We knew how things were because of Ellen's experience of serving with the mission and often being hungry.

Johnny came home and asked Mom to make a grocery list so he could buy food for the Weiss family. She wrote down some things like milk, flour and yeast, and then she looked up into her son's face and said, "We must put pepper on this list too!" At the time, I wondered what made her think that pepper was so important! She continued making quite a list of canned goods, as well as meat, rice and spaghetti, etc. As she handed Johnny the list, he went happily on his way to buy the groceries. *"Every man according as he purposeth in his heart, so let him give; not grudgingly, or of necessity: for God loveth a cheerful giver."* (II Cor. 9:7).

He had been correct in his guess that this young family was in need. That very morning, the Weisses had filled the baby's bottle with the last of the milk, and their cupboards were nearly bare. They knelt to pray, asking God to provide for their needs. When they got up from their knees, they saw a 50 pound sack of flour going by the window. The flour was on Johnny's shoulder, and he also brought in other boxes of groceries. The couple were extremely grateful and happy as they took things out of the boxes. Lois Weiss was ecstatic when she lifted the can of pepper out of a box. She exclaimed, "We have been out of pepper for months!" They thanked God for supplying their needs through the help of another caring Christian. It was a joy for our family also, that Johnny and my mother had been sensitive to follow the Holy Spirit's leading. Years later, we happened to turn on a Christian Radio Broadcast and heard George Weiss relating this incident just as I have written it here.

* * * *

I took typing, shorthand, bookkeeping and business letters as my elective subjects in my junior and senior years. Those were challenging and interesting studies. There were no quiet electric typewriters at that time, only manual Underwoods. The keyboards were blank so we were taught the finger positions and the keyboard characters by the instructor. Imagine the noise when thirty-six students began typing at once as the teacher was shouting: "fff space jjj space!" One would think her ears would be ringing, and her throat sore after several hours of that. She did have some shorthand classes too, which probably gave her ears and vocal chords a rest.

A month before my graduation, my brother, Karl, met with an accident. It was on a beautiful day, May 9, 1937. Karl was driving from Hibbing and stopped his pickup truck beside the highway to help another motorist repair a flat tire. He always had a kind heart, quick to help when he would see a need. After talking with the motorist, Karl walked back to his truck to get some tools. Just then a drunk driver swerved suddenly and hit him, smashing him against his own vehicle. It fractured both legs and one arm, and as he fell, the edge of the pavement scalped him so that blood gushed across both traffic lanes. Police, who had been following and attempting to chase down the drunk driver, took Karl to the hospital. The drunk got away. When we were notified of the accident, we drove ten miles to the Hibbing Hospital, but Karl had died at the scene of the accident, his life snuffed out at age 23. It was Mother's Day, and also Inger's birthday. I will always remember seeing my mother the following day with tears streaming down her cheeks, as she was pressing a suit Karl was to wear in his casket. Karl was buried under the pines in the cemetery by the Celina Church.

It was difficult for me to return to classes. I had been exhausted for a long time from the pressures of studying at all hours. Now there was also the emotional upset of a death in the family to deal with and make-up work to face at school. I had missed only two days of classes, but it took me two weeks to make up all the work. One instructor had gone to the funeral of her own brother at the same time as I was absent. I thought she would be understanding and sympathetic, but it was painful that she showed no mercy. If anything, she was stricter than the others. Of course, we were there to get an education and she did her best to see that we got it.

I did not sleep well after my brother's death. I had nightmares. One night, I thought I was awakened by the scraping and crunching of many shovels in the gravel of a road and when the filled shovels were lifted, blood ran from them. I awakened to find that reality was worse than the nightmare – my brother had died needlessly in the prime of life at the hands of a drunk driver, who killed and got away with it. Of course he doesn't really 'get away with it.' He will be accountable to God who sees all. *"God shall judge the righteous and the wicked..."* (Eccl 3:17a). In the meantime, God comforted our family in our grief. *"Blessed are they that mourn for they shall be comforted."* (Mt. 5:4)

A month later, I graduated with my class and felt better after I rested up.

\*   \*   \*   \*

That same year there were two weddings in the family. Inger married Clifford Stahl on March 5, 1937. Eight months later on November 5, 1937, Agnes married Wallace Stahl, Clifford's brother.

## Chapter 26
## FEEDING A HARVEST CREW
### By Helga

During the summer of 1936 Edward again worked in the harvest fields and then hopped on freight trains to go to the West Coast. Yes, he was finding work, but also he traveled primarily because he had a hunger to be on the move and see new horizons. Again I was praying for him, not only for his safety, but that perhaps he would get the "wanderlust spirit" satisfied and be ready to settle down. God did keep him safe, but as for the hunger to travel, that never left him.

In 1937, for the third summer, Edward headed for North Dakota to join a harvest crew. While he was working elsewhere in North Dakota, I personally found out what hard work it was for farmers' wives who fed the harvest crews. That August, Ellen asked me if I would work with her providing meals during the approximate week that threshing would be done at their farm. Ellen knew what to expect. The threshing rig was hauled from one farm to the next. Usually Edward's brother, John, did that. The cooperative threshing crew was made up of the farmers and their sons in the area. They all helped one another. There were the Sola boys, Thompson and his son, the Swenson boys, the Iversons, and of course Edward Gilbertson and his brother.

Sometimes after the threshing rig was pulled onto their farm, there would be several days of rain, delaying the harvest work. At such times there was no problem about feeding a waiting crew, because they all went home to wait for the weather to clear. The food, however, was another matter. They had no refrigerator, freezer, or even any locker plant to store it in. If they had bought a lot of meat, it would have to be canned. Ham and bacon could be kept in the basement for awhile. The baked goods would have to be used up or shared with others. Of course, when the rain quit, Ellen would begin baking again during the "drying up" day or two until the crew would return to run the waiting rig.

There was no delay the year I came to help Ellen. I was

PHOTO: Harvest Crew - A steam tractor (far left) is used to power the threshing machine.

glad to go there and be of help and they paid me well. Once the crew arrived, all was a buzz of activities. Horses filled every stall in the barn, and boys and young men in the work crew filled the hayloft. They brought their bedding rolls, and tossed them up into the loft, ready to unroll at night.

We had about ten men to feed. Breakfast was served at 6 a.m., dinner at noon, and supper at 6 p.m. Also, midmorning and midafternoon, we brought hot coffee and gallons of lemonade with sandwiches, and cookies to the crews out in the field.

Every day, breakfast consisted of bacon and eggs, fried potatoes, sausage, pancakes with syrup, boiled wieners, cooked oatmeal, stewed prunes and raisins, fresh fruit, hot biscuits, toast, coffee, juice and milk. Both dinner and supper were heavy meals such as fried chicken, turkey and dressing, or a beef roast, with mashed potatoes and gravy, fresh vegetables, salad, freshly baked bread and desserts. Daily, Ellen baked her own rolls and bread. She also kept a good supply of fresh cookies, cakes and pies.

Those young men worked very hard in the hot sun and were ravenously hungry every time. If it was 103 degrees outside, it was likely also that hot in the kitchen. The cooking was all done on a cast iron, wood-burning range. At all hours of the day, something was cooking.

Late at night, after cleaning up the supper dishes and starting some things for the following day, Ellen and I fell into an exhausted sleep. Surely the men slept well too, but we had fewer hours than they. We were up again at 3:00 or 4:00 in the morning. Ellen started the bread dough or rolls first thing, giving the dough sufficient time to rise before baking it. I, meanwhile, set the table, pumped water, squeezed the lemons and stirred up gallons of lemonade, brought in wood for the fire, carried up foods from where they were stored in the cool basement, and a myriad of other tasks. Between mealtimes, we made sandwiches, baked cakes or cookies, and started preparations for the next meal. Besides that, we were hard-pressed to get all the dirty dishes washed in time to set them back on the table again. We surely could have used a third person to help!

The men were grateful for all the good home cooking.

Around the table the young men carried on their usual banter. Since I was twenty and single, the teasing was often aimed at me. "Marry this gal and you'll feast like this all the time!"

I blushed, but went about my work. Their teasing usually gave me cause to retreat to the kitchen. I had no personal interest in any of them since I had no one but Edward Rostvit on my mind. Just one glance at his graduation picture would set my heart to beating faster.

That week was a merry-go-round of endless work, so Ellen and I were very relieved when the final day came to an end and the threshing crew moved on.

PHOTO: Edward Rostvit, 1935.

Helga Gilbertson, 1937.

## Chapter 27
## NEWLYWEDS AND A "COVERED WAGON"
### By Helga

The following August, 1938, Edward again planned to get a job with a threshing crew in North Dakota. He invited me along on the 300-mile trip, as I could spend the time with my sister and her family at Cooperstown, while he was away working. I enjoyed the weeks of visiting Ellen and Ed, and of playing with my nephew, Carl, who was three months old. Edward found work with some farmers in the Jessie area, and was able to come on Sundays to see me. When the harvest was finished, Edward returned, well-tanned from all his outdoor labors. That evening, he took me out for a ride. We stopped at a picnic area by the river. We were alone. The moon cast its rays across the water. It was there that Edward proposed to me. I accepted.

On our return trip, we stopped in Crookston, Minnesota, where Edward bought me a diamond ring and matching wedding band set. The price was $22, a high price for those hard times. We knew we could not plan our wedding until Edward could find full-time work. Jobs were scarce. By this time, he was living on the Rostvit homestead, doing some timber cutting from time to time.

*   *   *   *

That fall of '38, I returned to the old homestead to run the Nass Post Office for a few weeks until it could be officially closed. Cousin Albert and his family, who had occupied the place for five years, had just moved into their own newly built home about three miles away. The old home and store were vacant and more run-down than ever. Mice thought they owned the place. The roof leaked in numerous spots when it rained. As winter set in with its snow, it was drafty, cold and lonely. Kindhearted Uncle Joe, who lived nearby would occasionally stop in to see if I was all right. I appreciated his thoughtfulness.

One morning I had another surprise visitor. Edward came

walking in. He pulled up a chair close to the wood-buring cook stove where I had a fire going. As he related his adventure, I set about cooking some breakfast for him. It seems that my brother Johnny had secured a job at a logging camp up north. He had invited Ed along feeling sure they would hire him too. When they arrived at the camp, however, only Johnny was put to work. Edward wondered what to do. He was frustrated. He couldn't drive away with Johnny's truck, so finally he determined to walk the fifty-two miles home. As he set out walking, whatever aggravation or frustration he had felt, dissipated. He walked all through the night, following the snow-packed road. There was a full moon, and the scenery of snow-covered trees was a delight to him as he kept on the move. Moonlight glistened across the snow of open areas. At one point a wolf paused and eyed the lone trekker, but then slinked off into the woods. Later Edward spotted a deer emerging from the forest. He decided to lie down in the rut so that the deer would not see him over the snow bank. The deer slowly walked across the road right in front of him. Edward was tempted to reach out and grab a leg, but thought better of it, knowing he might get kicked in the head. As he gazed up at her, he could see the vapor of her breath in the cold air, and of moisture clinging to hairs around her mouth. The deer never saw him, and slowly continued toward the trees on the other side of the road.

Edward relished the memory of the close encounter and of the beauty of the long night's walk. He enjoyed this break from his long hike to sit by the stove and tell his story. After breakfast he left to walk the last ten miles to his homestead. I watched him go down the road until he was out of sight. Then, I was alone again with only the ghosts of my childhood past to keep me company.

It was a happy day for me when the post office officially closed. The Nass Post Office had existed for twenty-five years, (June 25, 1913 through December 14, 1938.) From then on, mail was delivered to Togo.

I was busy packing my things when Uncle Joe stopped by. With concern in his voice he said, "Some pranksters have just tipped over your outhouse, and I don't know if I will be able to get it back up for you." *Dear Uncle Joe, still watching out for me.* I told him not to be worried, as I would be leaving the following day anyway.

Not long after I moved back to Chisholm, Paul Rostvit bought our old homestead. He got permission from Mom and Dad to burn down the dilapidated building.

\* \* \* \*

My brother, Johnny, and his fiancé, Grace Hackey, beat us to the altar the next June, 1939. I, as her bridesmaid, wore pink. Edward was the best man as he was a great friend with both my brothers, Johnny and Ingvald.

\* \* \* \*

September 1, 1939, a war was started in Europe. Nazi Germany was bombing Warsaw in their invasion of Poland. By September 3, Great Britain and France declared war on Germany.

PHOTO: Left to right: Helga, Edward, Grace and Johnny

All the war news did not affect my world as I was nearing the time to get married.

Edward had finally landed a job at Rocklawn Dairy – and I mean it was steady work! He was paid $30 a month, plus room and board, but was expected to work fourteen hours a day, seven days a week. Ed was not lazy. He always did his best on any job. He was up at 4 o'clock every morning, first milking the cows, then bottling the milk, then driving the delivery route. By afternoon, he had varied jobs: shoveling manure, washing milk bottles, or doing farm work like hauling rocks out of the fields or cutting brush. Then came the afternoon milking.

We set our wedding date for October 8, 1939, thirteen months after our engagement. When we set the time for one o'clock Saturday afternoon, Ed's boss Nelson "generously"

PHOTO: Helga and Edward Rostvit, October 8, 1939.

let Edward off work at noon. Ed rushed through the morning's milking and delivery route. Then, he hurriedly showered, put on his suit and sped off to the church in Hibbing. He barely got there in time. In fact, his hair was still wet.

I wore a long white satin gown which I had ordered from a Montgomery Ward catalog for $2.98. My bouquet was of snapdragons and sweet peas. Inger, my matron of honor, wore an aqua gown and carried flowers similar to mine. Edward had bought the bouquets, which made them more special to me. Inger's husband, Clifford, was best man. We were happy that from the Persson clan, Aunt Sarah and Cousin Anna could join all of our family for our special day. After the ceremony, we went to a photo studio to have our wedding picture taken, as was customary at that time.

I could say our first home was a covered wagon. Actually, we had one of the earliest made camping trailers. "Covered Wagon" was what the model was called. Following the wedding, we towed our trailer to Beatrice Lake for the short time we had before Edward had to return to work. After that, we lived in

PHOTO: Our first home, the 14 foot "Covered Wagon."

the trailer parked at Rocklawn Dairy. Since Edward no longer needed the room and board, his wages were $75 per month. He worked hard, but conditions were rough, especially when there were personality clashes with the cocky son of the owner who made life miserable for the hired workers. Edward stuck it out longer than other men, but finally he, too, had to quit.

\* \* \* \*

In late November we parked the trailer in Hibbing. A part of the town was actually going to be relocated. The mining company that operated the open-pit iron ore mine beside Hibbing wanted to extract the ore that was under the town. All buildings of north Hibbing would be moved, or sold for demolition, with the mining company paying off the owners. Edward bought one of those buildings, an old grocery store, for one dollar! He was to tear it down. Weather was chilly. There had already been some snow, but Edward thought we could manage living in the trailer. It was equipped with a small wood-burning stove for heat. It would take only chunks of wood hardly any bigger than 4" square. My husband had grown tired of having to cut such small blocks of wood. He also did not relish having to get up many times in the night to put more wood on the fire, so he invented a way for that stove to burn oil. He placed a brick in the bottom and made a container which would drip old used motor oil on that brick at such a rate that the fire never went out. Edward was particularly pleased with his invention, so he could enjoy sleeping through the night.

Edward's dad, Ole, came to Hibbing to help with the demolition. He stayed with us. At one end of the trailer was a bed, at the other end, a booth that made into a bed. Once in the middle of the night, Edward awoke, hearing a scratching sound. When he got up to investigate, he noticed it was very cold in the trailer. That night the temperatures plummeted, causing the oil in the stove to congeal and get plugged up. The fire had gone out. Groping for a flashlight, he noted that the scratching sound was coming from his dad. He asked, "Pa, what are you doing?"

The walls of the trailer, not being insulated, were entirely covered with a heavy frost. Ole's hair was stuck to the wall, so he was scratching at it to get free. With his wry sense of humor, he said, "Oh, I just thought I'd like to go outside and get some city heat."

The demolition was a lot of work, but the two Rostvit men kept steadily at it to get the building taken down as quickly as possible. They did make some money. Since normal wages were a dollar-a-day, he felt he came out pretty good on this salvage job. The furnace alone sold for $20. Wagon loads of scrap lumber were sold for as little as fifty cents. Windows, doors, or good planks for flooring sold for more. When the job was done, we wintered at the Rostvit homestead, and Edward took some logging jobs. The "Covered Wagon" would have been too cold to survive in. When weather was warmer, if the timber cutting work would be farther away, we would take our trailer and park it in the forest near his work.

In the summer of 1940, we enjoyed a vacation, or a late honeymoon, to Yellowstone Park towing our little trailer. We saw Mt. Rushmore while it was still unfinished. Men who worked on the faces looked as small as ants, or perhaps spiders, since they were suspended from ropes. Our small '34 Chevrolet Coupe barely had enough power to pull our trailer up the steep grades of the Big Horn Mountains in Wyoming. Going on to

PHOTO: Helga by their '34 Coupe

Yellowstone, we marveled at Old Faithful and many other geysers, relished the beauty of Yellowstone Falls, and got sunburned as we walked to various steaming blue pools, or bubbling mud pots. We even enjoyed seeing the bears – as long as we could stay safely in our car.

    A few months later, another dairy in Hibbing, Island Farm Creamery, offered Edward a job he couldn't refuse. This meant less work hours and higher wages. He would no longer be doing any of the milking nor other farm chores. In this position, he only delivered milk and other dairy products to homes and stores. His cheerful disposition got him many new customers. He was happy to sign up new families or stores if they needed delivery service. It did add to his pay check. However, he refused to take customers away from other creameries. People respected him for that stand. The first time he received a pay check it was over $150 dollars, more than double what he had made at Rocklawn Dairy. He felt rich!

    The war, meantime, was escalating in Europe. April 9, 1940, Hitler occupied Denmark and Norway. On May 10, was the invasion of the lowland countries, Belgium and Holland. The Russian army, too, was bombing and harassing Finland. Other nations were in sympathy with Finland.

Grace & Johnny
'37 Pontiac

Helga & Edward
'34 Chevy Coupe

Inger & Clifford
with David
'28 Chrysler

Ellen & Ed with Carl
Ed's brother John

Wally & Agnes

Laura & Paul

Ingvald, Sanna
'35 Ford

## Chapter 28
## RAISING A FAMILY IN WAR TIME
### By Helga

By March of 1941, we had our trailer parked by my folks' place for it was time for our first baby to arrive. Through the months of my pregnancy, I had hoped the baby would be born on my birthday, just as my mother's firstborn, Laura, came on her birthday. My dream came true when our daughter was born March 31, 1941. My eldest sister, Laura, was so dear to me, that we decided to give our daughter the same name, but so as not to get confused with my sister, we always called our girl by both her names, Laura Jean.

When we left the hospital, we moved into an apartment in Hibbing, near the big open-pit mine. We paid ten dollars a month rent and that was a high price to pay. I was overjoyed that Edward had bought a nice used washing machine, a toaster and a console radio, as a surprise for me when I walked into the apartment the first time. On our radio we heard updates about the war on the European front. On April 6, 1941, the Nazis attacked Yugoslavia and Greece.

Earlier that year, Edward had received a draft notice, signed by President Roosevelt, with orders to go to Fort Snelling for a physical, which he did. For three days he stood in long lines for various tests, and was rushed from one area to another. At mealtime they were served mostly highly spiced foods which had to be eaten in a hurry, and Edward began feeling sick. When they had finished all the x-rays on the third day, they said, "You have ulcers! The army can't use you." They scrawled 4-F on all his papers and sent him home. The 4-F rating was for anyone who was excused from military service, be it for ill health, or for jobs considered necessary for defense – such as farming. Edward had had ulcers before, but had not had symptoms for over two years, so he was sure it had healed, but the army made him a sick man in a hurry. After that, Edward's ulcers got so bad that at times, he could not keep food down.

We also faced trials in our apartment. It was the second story of a lady's home. It wasn't anything fancy. It had glum, dirty walls in need of paint. The faded drapes and old furniture didn't add any cheer to the place either. We could have been quite happy there. After all, we had grown up in the Depression and were not used to having everything, but here we were all sick. The gas stove was an ugly antique with long black legs. There was a small gas leak someplace, giving the kitchen a peculiar sewer-like odor. Perhaps that was the cause of us being sick. The landlady, who lived downstairs, would do nothing about it. Then too, at night, we were often awakened by a lot of noise that sounded like the woman was dumping all her furniture upside down! We didn't trust her, so we always kept our door locked.

When the weather turned warmer, Laura Jean became fretful. She was developing a rash. I thought maybe I had kept too many covers on her and that she had heat rash, but then I discovered there were lots of bedbugs. Poor baby! That was 'the last straw!' We soon moved to a three-room rental house, a sunny, cheerful place. We no longer had to fear that unpredictably odd landlady, nor to be startled out of sleep by her thunderously loud and strange noises at midnight.

*   *   *   *

Every American was in a state of shock when the news came over the radio that the Japanese had bombed Pearl Harbor and that thousands of our service men were killed in the surprise attack. It was December 7, 1941. That same day, President Roosevelt addressed the nation, via radio, and called it "A Day of Infamy." The following day he declared war on Japan and her allies – Germany and Italy. There was much talk about the three leaders of those countries: Hirohito, Hitler, and Mussolini. The battle cry in every newspaper became, "Remember Pearl Harbor." Prime Minister Churchill came from England to spend several days having consultations with President FDR. They both spoke often on the radio. America was now embroiled in war on many fronts and our lives were changed entirely from that time on.

There was much sadness over the dead and missing at Pearl Harbor, and over the departure of young men leaving for war by the busloads. Crowds gathered in the streets, watching tearful goodbyes of parents, wives, and sweethearts who knew full well that some of those young men would never return alive. My brother Ingvald, and also Clifford, my sister Inger's husband, were drafted.

My mother had written a letter for Ingvald, her youngest son. She had written it back in 1937, not intending for Ingvald to read it until after her death. It's not that she had any premonitions that she would die soon. Now, however, with the prospect of Ingvald going to war, she thought it best for him to have it. She slipped him this letter as he was to leave town.

PHOTO 1943: Ingvald drafted for service in World War II.

*Dearest son Ingvald,*                 *June 21, 1937*

*I will here write you a few words, that you can read when I am gone. You know I gave myself to the Lord. He died for me and I asked him to forgive me my sins, and he did. I am in him and he will get me when I die, and "He that dwelleth in the secret place of the Most High shall abide under the shadow of the Almighty. I will say of the Lord he is my refuge and my fortress, my God, in him will I trust." Psalm 91:1-2 and please read the rest of this Psalm and give thyself to him, and do his will, Ingvald, not only Sundays but always. Be more afraid of the devil, his snares, and sin, than to lose your life.*

*I have prayed for you my children that you may come to the Lord and be true to him, but it seems at times that*

*Satan is stronger, but I know God is strongest. I have seen it many times, and he will win out, and when you come to the Lord, Ingvald, shun company of the unsaved. Don't be snobbish to them, but I mean don't be partners with them in anything, as they will lead you into worldly things. Remember, when you are saved, you are in the world, but not of the world. Jesus says, "I am come a light into the world, that whosoever believeth on me should not abide in darkness." John 12:46*

*We should not live in sin. "Keep thy tongue from evil, and thy lips from speaking guile." Psalm 34:13 You have always been a good boy, Ingvald, and I thank God therefore all my children has been good, and be good to Pa, and help him all you can. God will reward you.*

*Be honest, be upright and straight, in the smallest details as well as big ones. If you get a wife, be true to her. Don't let small girls or big take her place, and if you get girls of your own, remember they are a gift from God for you as their father to protect and love, but not as some say, that God has made them for the father to use in an adulterous way. That is the biggest sin a man can do, nearest to murder. But your character is not that low, and may God bless you my son in all you do. Thy children will respect you if you follow my advice.*

*Ingvald pray that God will take away your sin, and stand true to him. When you read this, I am home with the Lord.*

*May the Lord always guide you, Ingvald.*
*Lots of love from Ma*

Later, Ingvald wrote a letter home, thanking his Mom and saying, "I have done this." He also had a small booklet of the Gospel of John. In the back was a paper explaining the way of salvation with a place for a signature to indicate that its owner had accepted the Lord. Ingvald had signed it in pencil, and later had written over it in a firm hand with ink. It was a great comfort to Sanna that her youngest, like many of her other children, had put his trust in Christ.

Ingvald finished his training and was stationed in Texas. The following year while in Texas, he had a couple of bad spells. The first occurred one night when he was sent out on patrol and was later found unconscious. He underwent a battery of tests, but they could not discover the cause. After his next bad spell, the army gave him an honorable medical discharge and sent him home. Three years later, on Sept 30, 1946, Ingvald married a local girl, Alice Boyle. [Later it was discovered that Ingvald had intestinal problems from birth. Internal organs were jumbled, not situated like they should have been. When he was a baby, Mom had had a difficult time feeding him. He could only tolerate a very little at a time, or else he would violently throw it back up. Doctors said he shouldn't have lived to see his teens. He struggled with digestive problems all his life, yet he always had a very cheerful disposition.]

Clifford, on the other hand, went to Germany with his company and served many months there, before he was able to return home. Inger's family put a gold star in their window, as did many, to indicate they had a loved one overseas.

While Clifford was gone, his family had a struggle financially. They had two children, David and Betty. Inger was pregnant with the third. Somehow the Baptist Church in town got wind of their

PHOTO: Clifford and Inger Stahl
Children: David, Betty, and Donald

plight and brought boxes of groceries to them. Overwhelmed with gratitude, Inger and the children started attending that church and were faithful members there for decades. [In later years Betty became the church pianist. Others in the family sang specials.]

With the exodus of nearly every able-bodied man, women sought employment to fill the void and to help in the war effort. By the thousands they trooped into the shipyards and big factories to help produce more ships, planes, ammunition, and other necessities for defense and also for the home front. The music of the day reflected the times. Kate Smith often sang, "God Bless America." Equally popular were "Praise the Lord and Pass the Ammunition," and "Going Home on a Wing and a Prayer." (Many a brave young pilot having gone to battle never made it back to his base or aircraft carrier with his crippled plane.) Women employed in defense work inspired such songs as "Rosie, the Riveter."

With so many men away at war, a new joke became popular. It was made up of three words: "What a man!" "What, a man?" "What's a man?"

Many commodities or particular items were no longer on the market. Every six months we had to stand in line to get a coupon book allotted to us, according to the size of the family. Certain foods were limited: meat, cream, butter, coffee and sugar. We could not buy those foods at any price unless we had the coupon to go with it.

It was impossible to buy silk hosiery because that material was needed for parachutes. All ladies who had been accustomed to wearing seamed hosiery, now bought leg make-up and drew seam lines on the back of their legs. In this way, it appeared as if they were wearing silk stockings. The only problem was that it rubbed off on the bottom of the slip or dress, or stained the upholstery of furniture where they sat. About that time, Dupont developed nylon for the making of parachutes. Following the war they then also made nylon hosiery and other clothing.

Car factories were adapted to make trucks and tanks for

the war, so no new cars were coming off the assembly lines, causing the price of used cars to sky rocket. Before the prices had gone up, Edward had bought a new car. Only weeks later, a car dealer drove forty miles north to find us and buy that car back. He made us such a good deal that we couldn't pass up the offer. During the remainder of wartime, we managed with an old panel truck. It had been in an accident and Ingvald had fixed it up. For certain it was not the beautiful, nor comfortable vehicle we had before, but it was reliable. It always started faithfully even in the coldest time of winter.

Gas was limited and there were not enough gas coupons given for the average family to make it from one week to the next. They had to begin sharing rides to get to work each day. On Edward's creamery job, they were glad they still had the horses and enclosed wagons so they didn't have to use gasoline for their deliveries. However, the wagons had tires, and if one wore out, that was a real problem since rubber was another priority material needed for defense. Nothing containing rubber could be found on store shelves – not even a piece of elastic or a rubber band.

Edward got used to making his dairy deliveries with a horse and wagon. Besides saving on fuel, there was an advantage to this real horse power. Mainly, the horse grew accustomed to the route. Edward could carry the milk bottles he needed for two, three, or even four houses, walk from one to another and by then the horse had walked up the street to where he was. In the middle of the day Edward would stop at home for lunch, at which time he would let down the "anchor" on the wagon, which was a heavy circular piece of metal suspended from the front axle. In winter it was nice that there was no motor to worry about whether or not it would start again.

The disadvantage of using horses was dealing with their different temperaments. Bud, the first horse Edward had, always plodded along slowly and nothing Ed did could make that horse go faster. It was very annoying. Early one morning near the beginning of his route, Edward was already exasperated by Bud's slow pace. He picked up a handful of snow and formed

PHOTO: Edward drives a milk wagon.

a snowball to throw at the horse, "Get up, Bud!" As Edward flung the snowball, the horse was switching his tail. It happened that the snowball hit him in the rear. Just then, Bud clamped his tail down, holding the snowball there. It so startled him that he reared up, jerking the front axle and its two wheels out from under the wagon. Then he was off, running like the winged Pegasis with its two-wheeled "chariot" axle in tow. The anchor which resembled a manhole cover, clanked noisily, thumping up and down on the pavement, and as it occasionally hit the horse's heels, Bud only galloped all the faster. Off he went out of view. Thankfully the runaway occurred early enough, before work hours, that there was no traffic on the streets and no one was injured.

In the meantime, the front of the wagon had smacked down to the pavement, and the cargo of cases full of glass milk bottles were making a thunderous racket as they slid to the front of the wagon. Edward had leaped out of the wagon in time to avoid injury. The boss, Sven, brought Edward to our home. To their surprise, there stood Bud, huffing and puffing right in front of the house. He was accustomed to stopping there to rest while Edward would eat his lunch.

As Bud's problem had been his slow pace, Edward's second horse was the opposite. He was wild-eyed, skittish and always attempting to run away. With both extremes of horses, in time Edward taught them how to behave. It seemed whenever he had succeeded in training a horse, Sven would take it away to use it on another route, and in turn would give Edward another problem horse. Despite the exasperating times while having to train in the horses, Edward did love his job.

Sometimes, Edward finished his route by midday or at least by two o'clock. It took awhile for him to fill out his daily report. Each day he would turn it in to the creamery office with the money. When weather was good, he would spend the remainder of the afternoon fishing in a nearby lake.

One day in winter, as he was crossing an alley on foot, a driver lost control of his car on ice. Edward tried to hurry, but slipped and fell, injuring his back. He moved his legs to one side just in time to avoid being run over. He was troubled with back pain after that. When the creamery began using paper cartons in place of bottles, the cases were not as heavy to carry, which helped a lot.

**Ellen writes her view of the war years from their farm in North Dakota**

We had two children by this time: Carl born in 1938 and Elaine in 1940. The attack on Pearl Harbor happened when Carl was age 3½ and Elaine was 1½. That Sunday, we had driven over to visit Edward's siblings, John and Marie, and found them listening intently to the radio. That was when news of Pearl Harbor was being broadcast.

For our family and the farming area, the war had little effect. We put up a lot of our own food, canning

PHOTO: Edward and Ellen Gilbertson with Carl and Elaine

vegetables and meat. We had just bought a new set of tires before the restrictions came on. We also bought a heavy aluminum kettle because we needed it. There would be no more available when the supply ran out. Planes were needed more than kettles.

The year 1943 rolled around - two years after the attack on Pearl Harbor – and the war was still going on in Europe, North Africa, and across the Pacific. It seemed there would be no end to it, as island after island in the Pacific was being taken by the Japanese, and in Europe Hitler continued to stomp across the land.

The news depressed me, and the radio programs were even more depressing. As I sat in the darkened living room, while my husband listened to the radio in the dining room, I had a bad spell of pre-natal blues. Three-year-old Elaine came and put her arms around me – at least as far as her little arms would go. It was because of her and her brother and a third one who was not yet born, that I was depressed. What kind of a world were they going to inherit? Words of Jesus came to mind to soothe my troubled heart, *"These things I have spoken unto you, that in me ye might have peace. In the world ye shall have tribulation: but be of good cheer; I have overcome the world."* (John 16:33)

Our third child, Ruth Ann, was born on April 13, 1943. We had ration coupons but since we raised our own meat, eggs, vegetables, milk, cream and butter, we were never short of anything except sugar. Syrup for the baby's formula was one thing that was hard to get, but other relatives helped to get some when it was available. Except for our fears of what may happen, as I said, we were affected very little in our farming area, and of course, by the time our fourth child, Janice, was born in 1947, the war had ended.

**Back to Helga, writing about Minnesota:**

Around 1943, our daily routine was interrupted by an unusual turn of events. Edward suddenly remembered something

PHOTO: Laura Jean, Helga, and Ed Rostvit. 1943.

that had happened to him as a boy – and he wondered how he could have ever forgotten all about it!

Back in 1929 when he was twelve, Edward was out hunting for rabbits or partridge, armed with a 22 rifle. While he was wandering in the woods, he came upon what appeared to be the remains of an old root cellar. There was a depression where its sod roof had caved in. A narrow pipe was sticking out of the ground. With curiosity aroused, Edward laid down his rifle, took hold of the pipe, and pulled. It came up quite easily, causing dirt to filter down, revealing more of a hole. To his surprise the "pipe" was a very old long-barreled .45 pistol. Its octagon-shaped barrel was rusty. As he examined the gun, he wondered how long it had been since this place had been occupied, and by whom? Aside from the Minnesota Chipewa Indians, some of whom had been seen by the early homesteaders, trappers were the first white men to tramp through the North Woods to make their living.

Taking note of the hole revealed by the extracted pistol, Edward reached his hand down in and felt around. His fingers struck something smooth. He groped to get a grasp of it. Then he pulled out a cracked two-quart glass jar. His eyes grew wide to see that it was filled with folded paper money. Rather than the rectangular-sized bills of the day, the currency was mostly big, almost square bills, which had gone out of circulation in the mid-20s. Again he contemplated the question, *Whose money was this? Had a trapper hoarded a lot of money from selling pelts? Or had there been a robbery and the thieves had stashed their booty, using this dwelling for their hide-out from the law?* The questions would go unanswered. Now that he found this treasure, what was he to do with it? Not even knowing if he should mention it to anyone in his family, Edward decided to hide the jar until he could come up with a solution of what to do. He first extracted one of the big ten-dollar bills from the jar, and slipped it into his pocket. Then he went into one of the storage sheds on their homestead. Finding a loose floor board, he lifted it enough to ease the jar down between the floor joists. One day when his big brother Paul was driving into town, Edward rode along. As his brother busied himself gathering some needed supplies, Edward sneaked away and went to a bank to cash the bill for smaller change. He chiefly thought of buying candy. It would keep him supplied for some time – not only for himself, but also for slipping some candy bars into Helga's desk. Strangely enough, as time passed by, he had forgotten all about the jar of money.

Now some thirteen years later, Edward wondered if the money would still be there. He lost no time in making a rush trip back to the homestead at Bear River. By this time, no one was living on the place. He went straight to the storage shed and pried up the floor boards. The jar was there! Now that he had the treasure, which amounted to nearly $1,000 dollars, he again contemplated what to do with it. *Can I even cash these old style bills that have been out of circulation for nearly two decades? Would a bank be suspicious of someone cashing several at once? Would the law try to determine where it came from?*

Rather than taking all the money to the bank and possibly being questioned about it, Edward wisely filtered the bills into the money he collected on his milk route. When the first one was honored by the bank without question, he continued for months to filter the big bills into his route money. One day, he overheard his boss commenting, "I wonder who is paying with this old money!" Of course he didn't mind since the bank accepted them.

Our second daughter, Sharon Rae, was born on January 17, 1944. That spring we bought a home of our own in the Park Addition of Hibbing, a lovely area near a park. It was an attractive two-bedroom home with a full basement and a glassed-in front porch. The money that Edward found as a boy nearly covered the cost of buying the

PHOTO: Sharon (14 mo) Laura Jean (4 years), 1944.

home, which we got for a good price because it was still hard times.

I remember well the day of April 12, 1945. A newscaster interrupted a radio program to announce, "Fellow Americans! I regret to inform you that President Roosevelt is dead!" (He had died suddenly of a massive cerebral hemorrhage while he was at the beginning of his fourth term as president.) Our country was in turmoil, in a state of shock, grieving over the loss of our competent, well-loved, and respected leader. People wept openly upon hearing the news and wondered if there was another man who would be able to lead the nation as well as President Roosevelt had done.

At that time, I was expecting again. This pregnancy was different - I was getting cumbersome so early. My siblings assumed that this time, we would have a boy. When we would visit Paul and Laura, my sister would giggle and say, "Here comes that thing again!"

In mid-August, about the time that World War II was coming to an end, I went into false labor. A nurse who was checking me said, "If this is only one baby, I'll feel very sorry for you!" Two weeks later, about September 1, I had more false labor. This time, the doctor told me he thought he heard two heart beats. It was my first confirmation that I was carrying twins.

On September 14, 1945 we welcomed Janice Ann. Eight minutes later, Faye Victoria came into the world. Both babies were in good health. Now we were a family of six and there were not enough hours in a day for me. We had four little girls, all under the age of 4½ years. There were constant diaper changes. Sharon, at 20 months, was still in diapers too. It was time consuming to wash, hang out, and fold 200 diapers a week, along with the family wash as well. Meal making had to be squeezed in between the baby and child care and I was never caught up with all the dirty dishes that piled up on the counter top. Occasionally, Edward got home early from his milk route and he would help hang some of the wash so I could find time to fix lunch. It was difficult to even start cooking supper on time. I didn't want to be late with a meal, as Edward still had ulcers, and food always eased the pain.

For a while, we put both twins in a bassinet. Eventually, we bought them new cribs, costing $35 each. I was proud of those nicely varnished cribs with a colorful nursery decal on the end panels, but they didn't look new for long. Janice and Faye who were teething, gnawed like little beavers on the corner posts and all along the side rails. I worried that they would get sick from the bits of varnish they must have swallowed, but it didn't seem to bother them.

One weekend, when the twins were seven months old, my sister, Laura, took care of our girls while Edward and I took a break to go fishing. When we returned, she told me that the babies could sing. I didn't believe her. "Listen," Laura said, as she sang, "Don't let the smoke get in your eyes. Don't let the moon break your heart…" Faye and Janice were humming along with her. (Laura never could keep a tune very well. Maybe the twins thought she needed a little help.)

Laura Jean also sang at an early age, and Sharon, when only twenty months, heard someone singing "Little Sir Echo," and she sang all the echoes in the right places without being taught. We knew not then, but our four girls would eventually be singers.

## Chapter 29
## IN SICKNESS AND IN HEALTH
### by Helga

When Sharon was 2½ years old, she suddenly became ill. Her temperature shot up to 105. We feared that it might be polio since there was an epidemic in Hibbing. (At least, it was considered an epidemic when, in a few weeks, there were sixteen cases in the town of 16,000 population.) In fact, there were a lot of cases all over the U.S. in the hot months of July and August that year of 1946. Many people with lobar polio died, or were in an iron lung for the rest of their lives. It was very frightening since there was so little known about the disease at that time.

We took Sharon to the doctor and were relieved when he assured us that it was not polio. He explained that polio begins with a low-grade fever and neck pain, which Sharon did not have when he examined her. He gave us some medication for her, and sent us all home.

Two days later, Sharon tottered and fell when walking across the living room. She managed to get up, but fell again. On our way back to the doctor's office, she was holding a toy cup in her left hand. When she tried to take it by the handle with her right hand, she could not bring her pointer finger and thumb together. She looked puzzled. Setting the cup aside, she then tried to make her right hand cooperate by working it with her left hand. She was clearly baffled.

The doctor said it was polio after all. She was immediately admitted to the Detention Hospital since it was uncertain whether or not polio was a communicable disease. As I handed her to the nurse, Sharon said, "I cat walk." (She couldn't say the letter n.) I turned away with a heavy heart, wondering whether Sharon would recover completely, or be crippled, or be confined to an iron lung, or if we might even lose her!

We could not visit her during the two weeks she was in isolation, but after that, all the polio patients were moved to a temporary hospital ward set up in a big recreation building. It was a joy to visit her there. All signs of paralysis were gone and she was in good spirits. She was jumping around in her crib, laughing and singing. She cheered up the other patients who suffered crippling effects from the disease, and who were understandably depressed. One of the treatments was periodic hot packs applied to injured muscles.

PHOTO: Therapist with Sharon (age 2 ½) recovering from polio.

The hot packs were made from squares of woolen material, dipped in a warm solution. Sharon's packs didn't stay on very long. She used them as a ball, tossing them up in the air with a gleeful, "Whee!" Soon she was released from the hospital. For the next two years we had to take her periodically to a therapist for treatment.

[Sharon recovered well from polio except that her right leg was minutely shorter than the other. She needed to have her right shoe built up 1/8th inch to prevent a curvature in her spine. We thank God that she is not an invalid in a wheel chair, but can enjoy a normal life.]

*  *  *  *

During our eight years of marriage, our family had not been going to church. Of course in the beginning, Edward was working seven days a week. Then when he got the job at Island Farm Creamery, he didn't work on Sundays, but instead of going to church, he would go fishing with his friends. I was left at home to care for the children. Even if I had a car, I didn't know how to drive. In the late spring of 1947, when Ed and I were thirty, he taught me how to drive. The children were ages 7, 4, and 2. One day Edward said, "I suppose the children ought to be in Sunday School."

I didn't hesitate, but immediately said, "Yes, they should." From then on we attended as regularly as we could at the Christian and Missionary Alliance Church. I say "we," but Edward was not with us - only I and the children were attending. I would have liked for the whole family to go, but on Sundays Edward would sleep in, or would call one of his fishing buddies to pick him up on their way out to a lake. He later admitted that he felt guilty on those Sundays when he would be fishing instead of being with me and the children in church. He said, "I always remembered my mother saying, 'Sunday belongs to the Lord. We should be in the Lord's house.'" [As a boy on the Rostvit homestead they had attended the Bear River Lutheran Church, but services were not held every week. Reverend Fadum, who preached at the Celina Church near us, also preached on the same Sundays in Bear River, four miles from the Rostvit homestead. Ed had gone to church until he went through confirmation at the age of twelve. Then his mother died and the family seldom attended church after that.]

In 1947 we bought an older two-story, three-bedroom home on two acres at the south side of Hibbing. We had some remodeling done first and were overjoyed when our home was ready! I was delighted with everything. Best of all, compared to what life was like when growing up on the homestead, I appreciated having an indoor bathroom, a new furnace, and a full basement where I could hang clothes in the winter.

We were settled into our new home in time for Laura Jean to start first grade - riding on a school bus to get there. It was exciting for her. We didn't know that when the eldest child starts school, it is the signal for all the creepy crawly germs to invade the home. When Laura Jean got sick, whether it was a cold, the flu, measles, mumps, or chicken pox, the younger ones had to get sick too. They suffered bouts with tonsillitis besides all the other illnesses. I remember one time in particular, when they all were sick at once. Our bedrooms were upstairs, but I decided that it would be easier to take care of the children in the living room instead of running up and down stairs all day. I phoned the doctor. They still made house calls in those days. When he came, he found four little patients: one in each easy chair, and one at either end of the couch. He went to each and gave a shot while she was curled up in feverish sleep. There was an outraged scream of surprise each time the needle found its mark. It seemed such a cruel thing to do, but it was needful.

It had been a bad winter and when spring finally came, the doctor felt it would be best to perform tonsillectomies on all the children, whether or not they were flaring up at the time. Penicillin had just been discovered and at first was regarded as too much of a wonder drug, or cure-all. The doctor planned to do the surgeries following a three-day hospitalization with penicillin injections every four hours.

Their tonsillectomies were performed in one day. I sat and waited for the elevator to bring each one back to the ward

PHOTO 1948: The Rostvit Family: Helga and Ed, Sharon, Janice, Faye, and Laura Jean

after surgery. When their stretchers came out, they each looked so white, so little and defenseless. We took Laura Jean, Sharon and Janice home the following day. Faye was the youngest and the weakest. She had become so dehydrated that she looked like a little bag of bones in her blue sleeper. We feared we might lose her. She had to be fed intravenously and stayed in the hospital longer than the other three children. Our second winter in that home was a much better one with very little illness.

PHOTO: The twins, Janice and Faye, age 3

In early spring of 1949, Ed bought a '48 Chrysler Sedan. We liked the performance, comfort, and appearance, but the rear doors opened toward the front. We did not like that! One day, we decided to drive the 70 miles to Duluth, to shop. It was still cold, so the girls wore their snowsuits. On warm days some of the snow would melt, then refreeze at night so the shoulders of the roads were jagged and rough with refrozen ice, but the highway itself was clear and dry.

Later, as we were returning home, Faye was asleep in my lap while the other girls were playing in the back seat. As we came around a long outside curve at 65 miles an hour, suddenly there was a loud bang followed by the sound of rushing wind! Probably three-year-old Janice was playing with the knobs on the door, and must have been holding the door handle when the door flew open and threw her out. Edward slammed the brakes on so hard that I had a difficult time to keep from hitting the windshield with the sleeping child in my arms. (There were no seat belts back then.) Ed ran back to pick up Janice. He was frantic, assuming he would be picking up a dead child. Janice had tumbled in the jagged ice of the shoulder, and had narrowly missed hitting a metal sign post on that curve. Even as she was still tumbling, Ed noticed that her face was cut and bleeding. As soon as he reached her, he carefully picked her up. It was then that she cried. It was music to his ears to know she was still alive. The snowsuit she wore had been some protection from the sharp ice.

We weren't far from Duluth, so we turned around and went back to take Janice to the hospital emergency room. The x-rays showed no broken bones. Nevertheless, they admitted her for 24-hour observation.

We were all very quiet on the way home. Finally Edward said, "Poor Faye!"

I said, "That wasn't Faye. It was Janice." Either way, it was a sobering thought that we could have lost our little girl that day.

The following day when we returned to Duluth, hospital personnel notified us that we could take Janice home. They said she was all right except for bruises and scratches. When we entered the pediatric ward, we walked around, looking for Janice. We didn't recognize her, so we walked right past her crib. Then we heard a melody. We turned back. There was Janice, all black and blue. She had a bandage across her forehead, and her eyes were swollen shut. One foot was heavily bandaged, yet there she stood in her crib – singing!! I would say that was a good picture of obeying Scripture that tells us to, count it all joy when we fall into various trials. It's not easy to be joyful at the time of the trial, but at that moment we could have sung amid our tears. Ed gently lifted her out of the crib.

Upon leaving the hospital, Edward drove straight to the dealership,

PHOTO: Sharon, Laura Jean Janice and Faye, 1950.

229

and traded off that Chrysler for a new Buick with the dynaflow transmission. I won't expound on the questionable virtues of that car. It certainly did not perform like the Chrysler did, but suffice it to say, Edward refused to drive that Chrysler one more mile with those life-threatening doors. They became known as "suicide doors."

Janice had a sore foot and couldn't wear a shoe for a while. She wore a big rubber boot on that foot. Faye wore the other boot so she could look like her twin. From time to time we were reminded of her frightful experience as Janice would lift her sore foot and say, "Poor me, hey?" She wanted extra loving – and she got it every time.

*  *  *  *

Ed and I went to a Michigan factory and bought one of the first truck campers off the assembly line. It was called a Cree Coach. It did not have an extension over the cab as later ones did. At that time, Ed's ulcers were so bad that he had to take a two-month leave of absence from his job. It was 1952 when we took the family and drove to Alaska.

We traveled the famed Alcan Highway which was not yet paved. It was built jointly by Americans and Canadians during the Second World War. American military began construction at Dawson Creek (Milepost 0) and met the Canadian crew at mid-point. There was a celebration at that place, which is named Contact Point. The Alcan was a gravel road, rough and rocky in spots, and our truck's tires were slashed to ribbons by rocks in the road bed. Ed had to change a lot of flat tires. When it was sunny, dust was stirred up by traffic ahead of us, and when there was rain, it was all mud!! At one point, we had to wait with other motorists while highway workers laid planks for us to cross a stream where a bridge had washed out.

We saw a wayside restaurant that sported a big sign: EAT HERE IF IT KILLS YOU! WE NEED THE MONEY! We stopped to get some pop and it was 25 cents a bottle. At that time, it was a nickel a bottle in the States. When there was a store, we bought milk to calm Edward's ulcers, but many times the milk was sour so it didn't help.

Our Cree Coach worked out well for us. Whenever it was time for me to prepare a meal, the children enjoyed playing outside. Edward usually headed out with a fishing rod. The problem was that with being so far north, it would stay light until 10 o'clock and Edward would sometimes lose track of time and return late for supper. After eating, the booth would be made into a bed where Edward and I slept. Above that there was a pull-out canvas cot where eleven-year-old Laura Jean slept. The younger three: Sharon, 8, and the Twins, 6, slept in sleeping bags on the floor. When everyone tracked in mud all day, the hardest thing was cleaning the floor to put the girls to bed.

Gas was very high on the Alcan – up to 70 cents a gallon, while it was 20-25 cents in the States. After 1,400 miles of dust, rocks, or mud, we got onto a wonderful tar road. As the highway improved, so did the view. After having driven endless days through burned timberland and tundra, now there were beautiful glaciers and spectacular snow-capped mountains.

After seeing Anchorage, a small town that was growing too fast, we went to the coast where we were close to Russia. We saw a number of moose as we drove along. They appeared clumsy and awkward as they lumbered along, flopping their legs as if they were not joined together properly. We headed for Fairbanks, but a bridge was washed out. It would have been a long delay, so we headed homeward instead.

We got home after being gone two months. Shortly afterward we heard through our Christian and Missionary Alliance Church that a missionary family, the Thompsons, were going to Cambodia and needed a truck to ship over there. Edward then sold the truck and Cree Coach to them. [Decades later we learned that they used and used that truck, traveling over the worst of roads to do village evangelism, and that they would stay in the Cree Coach while in a village. They were very grateful to have a dependable sturdy truck for the tough work. We were glad to know it had been useful for the Lord's work.]

Edward returned to work, but he was still sick, often unable to keep food down. At that time, there was only one cure for ulcers – major surgery. In late January, 1953, surgeons did a 4-hour operation and removed nearly three-quarters of his stomach. He began recuperating, but he had to be on IVs for a long time to allow the stomach to heal. One day, while Ed was in the hospital, our girls went sledding near home. Janice, age 7, fell off the sled and lay screaming in pain. At first I didn't know who to call. There were no ambulances in Hibbing at the time. Then I thought about Ron Carlson, the pastor of the church where we had been attending five years. He came and carried Janice to the car and brought her to the hospital. Janice's right thigh bone had broken, having snapped very easily because of a cyst in the heart of the bone. Since the bone had broken at an angle, traction was needed to hold the bones in the proper position for healing. A steel pin was driven through the bone just below the knee. When the traction apparatus was in place, Janice was no longer in pain.

To compound my trials, my mother, at age 69, was also then admitted to the hospital. She had been ill for some time with uremia. She was terminal with cancer in the liver and other organs, so this was to be her final hospital stay. Doctors didn't think she would last more than a few days, but she clung to life.

I was 35 years old at this time, and was glad that Ed had taught me how to drive. It was no problem for me to be at the hospital during the day, since the other daughters were all in school, but, if I went in the evening, I had to hire a sitter. I didn't want the children at home to feel neglected and lonely, yet I needed to be with those who could not even get out of their beds of pain – all three of them. It would have helped if I could have taken the other children to the hospital with me, but that was against the hospital's regulations. No children under twelve were allowed to visit. At times, the burden seemed more than I could bear. I felt pulled in all directions. I did not know how to divide up my time between the children at home and my loving husband, my little girl in traction, and my dying mother in the hospital. Only God's grace sustained me.

As Valentine's Day drew near, I brought Janice some colored paper, glue, and scissors, so she could make valentines. She was her usual cheerful self and didn't complain when I said it was time for me to leave. As always she smiled and waved when I left her. That day, after I walked down the hall a ways, I remembered something and returned to her room. I found Janice in tears. Every day she had been brave and put up a good front for me when I left her. It was hard for her to lie in one position both day and night while in traction, and I'm sure that she wanted so much to be home. Most of all, she missed her twin. They have always been inseparable. How could I comfort my little girl in her pain and loneliness? As I drove home afterwards, the tears kept flowing. I had to stop the car because I could not see to drive. I prayed as I wept, and the God of all comfort calmed my aching heart.

After Janice had been in traction for three weeks, x-rays showed that the bones were beginning to knit properly. She was then encased in a body cast from the arm pits and down the one leg to her toes. It was to be left on for six weeks. When the cast dried, they placed her on a stretcher and took her to her daddy's room, so they could see each other before she would leave the hospital. Reverend Carlson was there to help me again. He carried Janice out to the car, and also into our home. He was of slight build, and I'm sure it was a cumbersome burden for him, but he had a compassionate heart. Janice adored him. Her sisters were very happy to see her, especially her twin who said, "Oh Janice, Janice!" then burst into tears. Janice was glad to be home again in spite of being in a cast. The inconvenience or discomfort never made her cross. She felt she had freedom compared to being flat on her back with her leg in the traction sling. One day I found her standing up. I couldn't understand how she accomplished that, but she was all smiles! Minnesota's school system had a tutor who gave Janice her school lessons each day at home so she didn't have to fall behind in her studies.

Edward got home just a few days after Janice did, so we had our whole family all together. Ed was only 120 pounds when he came home. Then not long after getting home, he developed phlebitis -a blood clot- in his leg. He was in extreme pain. Our pastor again came to the rescue. He carried Edward down the stairs and out to the car to take him back to the hospital. This dear preacher must have begun to think that his calling was to carry our family's sick members to and from the hospital.

[Pastor Carlson's compassion did not go unnoticed. The following year when our family moved to Colorado Springs, Colorado, it was Edward who wanted to seek out a church for the family. We attended as a family from then on, and in time each of our children, and Edward himself, made a public profession of faith in Jesus Christ as Lord and Savior. Each was also immersed in believer's baptism.]

Ed got home again a week later, but it took a long time before he felt well enough to go back to work.

I continued to make frequent visits to the hospital as my mother was still gravely ill. Lingering with her cancer and other complications, she lived three more months before she was released from her suffering.

## Chapter 30
## END OF AN ERA
### by Helga

Our dear mother died on June 14, 1953. We were thankful to have been raised by a godly woman. Many of her children and grandchildren as well as her brothers, Andrew and Krist, were present at her funeral, which was held in the church at Celina. She was buried under the pines in the church's cemetery, near the grave of her son, Karl. The house near Chisholm to which we Gilbertsons had moved when we left the homestead in 1933, had continued to be our parents' home. After Mom's death, Dad lived another decade. Sometimes he left Chisholm and would stay in his cabin by Blackduck Lake.

For a while my brother Johnny and his family also lived in a nearby cabin on the lake. Work was scarce. Dad had his saw rig set up there so the two of them could cut and sell lumber.

On Sundays Johnny's family held their own church service in the cabin. Johnny played guitar, and Grace the harmonica as their four girls: Joanne, Beulah, Marilyn, and Carolyn sang along. They also had drills of who could find Scriptures the fastest. Carolyn, age 3, was proud that one time she was the first to find John 3:16. Johnny would give a Bible lesson.

The three oldest girls attended a school across the lake. Johnny took them there

PHOTO: John and Sanna Gilbertson

each day by boat. One morning they awoke to a heavy rain. Before they left for school, they all bowed to pray. Six-year-old Marilyn who was only in kindergarten, prayed that God would keep them dry on the way to school.

Johnny had to smile at the child's "innocent" prayer. It was sweet of her to pray that way, but he felt sorry for her, envisioning that she would be in for a disappointment. As they crossed the lake, Johnny was the one to be in total amazement. Rain fell all around them, but in their rowboat they were bone dry. He dropped the children at school. On his return across the lake, Johnny got soaked! He couldn't wait to get inside and tell his wife about Marilyn's faith – and of his lack of it.

Their family lived by the lake through the winter too. Often, we went to visit them. Their daughters and ours were close to the same ages so they all had fun together. Edward would plow the snow off the frozen lake and all would enjoy ice skating. Then a chain of sleds would be attached behind the tractor and he would pull everyone around on the ice. The girls would squeal with delight, and we all laughed to see my dad "grandpa" getting the wildest ride on the last sled.

In Dad's last months when he was terminally ill with cancer, he stayed with my sister, Inger's family in Chisholm. They gave him loving care. Betty, who was a nurse, daily gave back rubs, and spoon fed him. Their godly example around him, as well as visits from the pastor of their church who spoke Norwegian, had a great impact on him. Before his death in June of 1963, Dad humbled himself and acknowledged his need to put his faith in Jesus.

PHOTO: Stahl family
Back: Clifford, David, Inger
Front: Don, Gloria, Ken, and Betty

*We, the children of the immigrants made our own lives in America. Here is a capsulated summary of the eight siblings:*

**Laura** stayed the nearest to our home place. She and husband Paul Rostvit, raised three children: Joan, Gregory, and Gale, on a farm near the Rostvit homestead, about ten miles west of Nass. In addition to his farm work, Paul also did some logging, and for thirty years he drove a school bus for Togo. Every Sunday they attended the Sturgeon River Chapel where Ellen had served for a time during her missionary labors with Northern Gospel Mission.

**Johnny** and Grace had five daughters: Joanne, Beulah, Marilyn, Carolyn, and Ruth Ann. Johnny had a kind, gentle nature. He enjoyed his work, whether logging, mechanics, or farming. For nearly a decade they were living a rugged pioneer existence in a coastal area of Alaska where he ran a saw mill. In winter only three families lived in secluded Auke Bay. On Sundays they all worshiped together - the owner of the saw mill leading the service.

**Ellen** and Edward Gilbertson raised four children: Carl, Elaine, Ruth, and Janice, on their farm in Cooperstown, North Dakota. Ellen also had a ministry, as she often was called upon to speak for ladies' meetings and other functions, not only in their church, but also in other churches of the area. She continued to write as well, publishing articles, short stories, and books.

**Karl** is in glory, having been taken to his eternal home early in life.

PHOTO: Gilbertson family
Back: Ellen, Carl, Edward
Front: Janice, Ruth, Elaine

**Inger** and Clifford Stahl raised their family in Chisholm. Clifford was a miner and worked some in Greenland, then in Liberia, Africa. Despite hardships, each of their five children paid their way through college. David drove public buses in Minneapolis and received commendations for 35 years of perfect, accident-free driving. Don was great in sports. He became a coach and also a high school principal. He was well qualified with four degrees, but his true gift was natural. He really had a way with youth, helping to channel lives in godly directions. Ken, the youngest of the sons, likewise was a high school principal. Both daughters Betty and Gloria, became Registered Nurses. Betty even served two terms in Viet Nam, tending the wounded. She had harrowing experiences yet her faith in God was a witness to others.

I, **Helga**, and Edward Rostvit with our four daughters: Laura Jean, Sharon, Janice, and Faye, moved to Colorado where Edward helped build the Air Force Academy and then became a millwright – precision work with setting up machinery. I became a Licensed Practical Nurse and our eldest daughter, Laura Jean, was a Registered Nurse. Our family was very involved with our church. I enjoyed serving with a ladies ministry, making things for orphans, or lap robes to be used in nursing homes.

Our daughters, while teenagers, formed a quartet, made recordings and traveled throughout the United States giving concerts in churches. After the two older ones married, the twins attended Bible college, then had a career of singing internationally. They ministered in ninety countries, singing or giving concerts in 116 languages.

**Agnes** and Wallace Stahl moved to Oregon for logging work there. They had two sons and two daughters: Beverly, Wallace Jr., Victoria, and Glen.

**Ingvald** and wife Alice never had any children. For many years they traveled with the Holiday on Ice Show. Ingvald ran the ice machine, while Alice sewed costumes for the skaters. Later they made their home in Michigan, where Ingvald again enjoyed mechanic work, keeping a fleet of trucks on the road. Because of his intestinal disorders, he died at age 57.

PHOTO: Rostvit Sisters Quartet: Faye, Laura Jean, Janice, Front: Sharon

PHOTO: Rostvit Twins Faye and Janice

\* \* \* \*

We no longer live in the horse and buggy days, nor even in the days of the Model T when a 100 mile trip was a long ways to go. With the improvements of transportation, American families have scattered across the country. Our family was no exception. We, too settled in different areas, but we loved one another and kept in touch. We often made trips to Minnesota to visit the relatives who were there. I still loved picking and canning wild blueberries. Edward enjoyed fishing in the summer, or snowmobiling in the winter. The last trip we made to the north while Edward was still able to drive, was in 2004. We were age 87. We visited with family and friends in various towns. One day we drove northward to the area where we had grown up on homesteads. We drove by the Rostvit homestead, and saw a man planting trees out in a field. Edward shook his head and laughed. "It's ironic. My dad

PHOTO: Uncle Andrew and Aunt Sarah in their later years sitting by the Persson Homestead cabin.

worked hard felling the timber, then grubbing out the stumps to clear that field for planting, and now someone turns it back into a forest."

Going farther north and east, we turned off the county road, driving up the long winding lane into the old Persson homestead, my Uncle Andrew and Auntie Sarah's place. Their youngest son - my cousin Hilding who never married - still lived there in a small home. He had recently turned 92. When we drove up, Hilding was sitting on a bench by the weather-beaten logs of the original homestead cabin. Its roof had long since caved in. We tried to imagine the family with ten of their eleven children living in this two-room home, with its attic-bedroom.

Our twin daughters, Janice and Faye, were with us so they relished seeing the old homestead site. Hilding showed them the old barn. Its roof had also caved in with some past winters' heavy snows. There was a woodshed, some other log out buildings, as well as Hilding's former garage. It was on the verge of falling down – leaning at about a 45 degree angle. Poles had been propped against one outer wall, but it was uncertain how long they could prevent the inevitable collapse. The twins ducked to peer through its sunken doorway. Surprised to see tools still hanging on the walls, Faye turned and asked, "Hilding, do you still go in there?"

He shifted from one foot to the other and scratched his head. With a twinkle in his eye and a wry grin, he slowly said, "Oh, ya, but I pray first."

From the Persson homestead we made our way eastward to see the place where I and my siblings grew up on the Skoglie (then Gilbertson) homestead. With our store/post office and home building having been burned down years ago, the old home place had returned to the wilderness state it once was in before the arrival of the immigrants a century ago. We found evidence of some charred logs in the center of the meadow where the first post office had once stood. From there we angled our way toward my grandparents' homestead, perhaps the approximate route my older siblings and Dad had made that snowy March morning when I was born. In the location where Grandpa Jonas' cabin had been, I came upon an old coffee pot.

I picked it up and thought of my Grandmother Kristina being up before dawn with coffee already on the stove the day of my birth. I thought of my mother in her twenties, boiling some coffee over a fire in a hollow stump when their homestead cabin was first being built. Then there was the winter when they ran out of coffee and other staples when the store ten miles away had burned down. I thought of my mom and Auntie Sarah often having enjoyable chats over a cup of coffee.

All that our parents and grandparents worked for was gone – all their sweat and toil to develop their homestead, and now it was overgrown with trees, brush and weeds. Likewise, one would never know where our one-room school had once stood.

We went on to the Celina Cemetery at twilight. Darkness was falling fast, but the moon was rising. We visited the graves of both sets of my grandparents, but we had to use a flashlight to read the engraving on the headstones. We also paused to see the granite stones on the graves of my brother, Karl, and of my parents. They were courageous, God-fearing people. When they left their homeland and traveled to a far away country to homestead in America's wilderness, they depended on God's promise and found it to be true, *"The Lord Thy God is with thee whithersoever thou goest."* (Joshua 1:9) They learned that God was bigger than their strengths or their weaknesses, bigger than their accomplishments or their failures, bigger than their wildest dreams or their dashed hopes, and big enough to sustain them through trials, and beyond tragedies.

With the passing of our immigrant parents and our grandparents, an era was ending - the era of Minnesota's immigrants, of the homesteaders, of the pioneers in the wilderness of the North. By their hard labors, the following generations would benefit. We all have it easier now. Aside from the physical benefits, there were social benefits. We gained from their example of being good honest citizens, of working hard, and of helping neighbors and strangers. They also guided us spiritually. They planted seeds of hope, of kindness, of love, of faith in Jesus Christ, and of trust and dependence on God in all situations. We, their children and their children's children, have reaped the benefits.

If we were only to look at the homesteads which had returned to their former wilderness state, we could conclude that our parents' and grandparents' labors were in vain, just as when King Solomon looked on all the works that his hands had done and concluded that all was vanity and grasping for the wind.

In reality, there was something far more important than to keep the physical evidence of our forefather's labors in the North Woods. No one can take anything with them when they leave this life. The example of their faith is the best thing that they could leave, and they left that in our hearts. *"One generation shall praise Thy works to another, and shall declare Thy mighty acts."* (Psalm 145:4)